JONAH:
RESPONDING TO GOD IN ALL THE RIGHT WAYS

JONAH:
RESPONDING TO GOD IN ALL THE RIGHT WAYS

HAL SEED

IF YOU THINK YOU KNOW THE STORY OF JONAH, THINK AGAIN!

Called by God to reach the Ninevites, Jonah runs the other way, triggering a cosmic dilemma: what does God do with a wayward prophet? In four short chapters, God proves His greatness and grace by redirecting, restoring and then using Jonah. He sparks an evangelistic fire never before seen in history; an entire city turns to God.

Jonah: Responding to God in All the Right Ways is designed as a four-week spiritual experience that can be used:

- Individually, with four weeks of daily readings.

- With a small group, using the weekly discussion guides.

- In a church-wide campaign, accompanied by web-accessible sermons.

Jonah will enrich your time with God, help you understand the "Twin Peaks" of His character, lead you in a daily response to His greatness, and motivate you to want to serve Him more fully. Specifically, you will learn:

- How God disciplines His children

- How fear can be turned to faith

- How to pray when in deep distress

- How to keep a tender heart toward God

- How to become a great question-asker

- How God gives second chances

- How to memorize Scripture

- How God feels about the least lovable people

- How God teaches His servants

- How to respond to God's greatness and grace

Seed, Harris W., III, 1957—

Jonah: Responding to God in All the Right Ways/Hal Seed

ISBN-13: 978-0-9797878-3-6

ISBN-10: 0-9797878-3-1

Also by Hal Seed:

The God Questions: Exploring Life's Great Questions about God

Future History: Understanding the Book of Daniel and End Times Prophecy

To purchase copies and for other books, CDs, articles and free resources, visit www.halseedbooks.com.

Jonah is dedicated to Chuck Riffe, Dennis DeMille, Don Kuhn and Scott Evans, the men of my small group, who helped test and refine the Bible Discussions as well as test and refine *me* in our weekly times together. How good and pleasant it is when brothers live together in unity!

I am indebted to Kim Bilas, Toni Ridgaway, Alexia Wuerdeman, Jan Funchess, Lisa Frost, Eric Vasilades, and Dirk Currier, a stellar team of servants who enable resources to flow from *The Church Next Door*. If you benefit from the word choices and easy-to-read format, thank Kim, Toni and Alexia. Dirk Currier and his church field-tested the book as a Church-Wide Campaign. If you listen to CDs or utilize our PowerPoint presentations, thank Jan. If you found out about this resource or accessed items from www.halseedbooks.com, thank Lisa and Eric. Of deep significance to me is my wife Lori's contributions to the quality of the text, and my daughter Amy's contribution of the *Afterword*.

Contents

How to Get the Most Out of This Book

Jonah: Responding to God in All the Right Ways was written to help you understand the book of Jonah and apply what you learn by responding to God in new and appropriate ways every day. The book is structured with five daily readings and a Discussion Guide for each chapter of the Book of Jonah.

Ideally, you'll follow the daily readings Monday through Friday, take Saturday off, and go to church on Sunday. If you're part of a small group, you'll meet with your group sometime during the week to go through the Discussion Guide for that chapter.

Each Daily Reading concludes with the question *"How Do You Respond to a God Like That?"* followed by suggestions or guidance relevant to that day's topic. Jesus said, *"Everyone who hears these words of mine and puts them into practice is like a wise man who built his house on the rock"* (Matthew 7:24). My prayer is that you will become a more authentic responder to God at every turn as a result of your experience with this book.

INTRODUCTION

The story of Jonah is one of the best-known stories in history. Both people who attend church and those who don't attend are familiar with it. Stop ten people on the street and ask, "Have you heard the story of *Jonah and the Whale*?" and nine of them will say, "Yes." This is slightly humorous, considering there is no whale in Jonah's story. A whale is a mammal; the Bible says Jonah was swallowed by a "big fish." But there's a real irony of the story of Jonah: *the story isn't about Jonah*. The story of Jonah or, more properly, the Book of Jonah is about *God*.

Think of the book as a screenplay. Jonah is a supporting actor, and God is the hero and main character. *God* is the star of this four chapter novelette in the middle of the Minor Prophets. I've written this brief book because I want you to see God for who He is. Once you've seen Him through the eyes of Jonah, you'll never see or think of Him in the same way again. My hope is that by seeing the right and wrong ways Jonah and others respond to God, you'll more easily find and choose the right ways for yourself.

You are beginning a four-week adventure into one of the great stories of history. Along the way, you'll encounter wind, waves, worms and one very reluctant prophet. Watching over all of them is a great and grace-filled God. As much as any book in the Bible, the Book of Jonah showcases God's two most important qualities: *greatness and grace*. I'll explain why these are so important a little later. For now, let me paint you a picture.

Photo Taken by Jill Otis

My children were born in Longmont, Colorado. Longmont is a quiet city at the base of the Rocky Mountains. Wherever you go in this perfect little town, your view is dominated by two mountains:

Longs Peak and Mt. Meeker. Together, these mountains are called, "The Twin Peaks." Visit Longmont and you'll agree: they're aptly named. Longs Peak and Mt. Meeker are towering compliments to each other. Individually, they're impressive; together, they're breathtaking.

The Book of Jonah has its own Twin Peaks. God's lofty traits of greatness and grace tower over every chapter of the book. By themselves, God's greatness and grace are both impressive. Together, they're everything a creature could hope for in his or her Creator. Chapters one and two major in God's greatness as God demonstrates His power over nature. Chapters three and four focus on His grace as He demonstrates His willingness to forgive.

My family doesn't live in Longmont anymore; we're beach bums these days. Still, I will never forget those peaks. By the time you're through with Jonah, I have a hunch you won't either.

How to Use Jonah as a Small Group Study

Jonah was designed to be used as a four-week small group experience and/or church-wide campaign. I have written five devotional readings plus a Discussion Guide for each of the four chapters of the Book of Jonah. Ideally, you'll hand out books one week prior to your first small group discussion, and each member will read the five devotions for Jonah 1 before discussing chapter one, repeating the process each week thereafter.

I have five strong convictions about small groups:

1. Life is sweeter when it's shared with others. The highs are higher, and the lows aren't as low.

2. Iron sharpens iron. Life-change happens best in the context of a small group of trusted friends.

3. God sometimes speaks through the voice of a good friend.

4. The most important meeting of the church is when it gathers for worship and teaching. The second most important meeting is when community happens.

5. Community, by definition, means *knowing and being known, loving and being loved, serving and being served, celebrating and being celebrated*.[1]

Small groups stimulate you to deeper intimacy and spur you to greater accountability with one another. Each Discussion Guide begins with a question designed to loosen up the group and help you get to know each other. Don't skip this question! It will help you bond, which will make all the difference in your sharing. If your group members become close, there will be days when you won't get to the discussion, because someone in the group will have a critical question or issue that needs attention that day. In my experience, those are some of the best days your group will have. If you are not already part of a small group, I hope you will use the resources of *Jonah* to inspire you to develop or join one.

---

[1] Bill Hybels taught me this.

How to Start a New Group

If you're not currently part of a group, here's how you start one:

1. *Decide what time and day will work best for you.* One key principle of a small group is that the leader must attend almost all the meetings. Commit to a time and place and prioritize it in your schedule.

2. *Decide what kind of group you'd like to have.* Personally, I prefer to be in a men's group. I find that men open up better without women present. I suspect the same is true for our female counterparts. Single folks might prefer to be in a mixed-gender group, and married folks might like to have their spouses present. Decide what will work best, and then make a list of four to six people who fit that profile and who you'd like to get to know better.

3. *Call and invite people to join your group.* Say, "Hi_____! I just found this paperback on the book of Jonah. It's called *Responding to God in All the Right Ways*, and it looks really good. I'd like to do a group study on it. Would you like to join me?"

4. *Stop inviting when you've got four or five in your group.* Groups can *become* larger than that, but if they start larger than that, it will take members longer for them to connect with one another. It is better to start with four to five and later invite additional people after you've been meeting for a few months. (My current group started with just three of us.)

5. *Bring enough books for everyone to the first meeting.* If you're not sure how many will be there, make a photocopy of the first chapter, promising to have the "real thing" for them next week.

6. *Introduce yourselves, remind the group of why you're meeting, pray and begin the discussion of chapter one.* It's that simple. Don't ask for a long-term commitment; if the study goes well, it will come naturally.

7. *Call anyone who misses the group and see how they're doing.* Everyone likes to know they're missed. Call and find out if they're O.K., see if they hope or plan to come next week, and let them know you want them there.

How to Use Jonah as a Church-Wide Campaign

Church-wide campaigns can have a powerful effect on an entire church. When Dan Grider and I wrote *The God Questions*, it surprised us how powerfully our church members (and church attendance) grew during those campaigns. Dan often says, "The sun can warm you, but a laser cuts through steel." He means that when you focus light in a single direction, it becomes much more powerful. We found a palpable difference between the impact of a normal sermon series and a sermon series where everyone in the church is studying the same material. For maximum growth and impact, I believe pastors should try to focus the entire church—its sermons, readings and small groups—on a single subject at least once or twice a year. The richness of the mutual learning, interpersonal relationships and discussions is far superior to studying one topic on Sunday, a second topic in your personal devotions, and a third topic in your small group.

We've developed *Jonah* with all the tools you need to create an all-church campaign. Your pastor can order full-length, adaptable sermon manuscripts and message notes templates for inserting in your church bulletin from www.halseedbooks.com. We'll even give you the cover artwork to use in your services. Everything else you need for the campaign is included in this book.

How Does a Campaign Work?

Much like a capital funds campaign, a topical campaign requires a little (though not a lot) of advanced planning. Usually campaigns work better in the October–December or late January–April time frame; those are the times when most church members consistently attend. *Jonah* is an especially flexible campaign because of its length. You might even consider using it as a short summer series or a quick post-Easter campaign leading up to Mother's Day.

Following are the simple steps from start to finish for a successful church-wide campaign.

1. **Six weeks ahead:** Make the final decision to hold the campaign. Order books, sermon CDs and/or message manuscripts, plus message notes templates.

2. **Five weeks ahead:** Alert your weekend program or service planning team about this special series. They will want time to plan appropriately for special music, programs and/or artwork. They may even want to do some extra decorating around the church.

3. **Four weeks ahead:** Make an excited announcement to the whole church. Showcase Jonah artwork and make the books available for those who want to read ahead. Include a small group sign-up sheet in your church bulletin and host a table for people to register for small groups and/or volunteer to be group leaders.

4. **Three weeks ahead:** Hold an orientation huddle with your staff and small group leaders. Information is power. Be sure they know what Jonah is all about and why you're holding the campaign. Continue taking small group registrations.

5. **Two weeks ahead:** Post or publish small group rosters, allowing room for those who still haven't signed up. Encourage members to invite their friends to the first sermon of the series and to their small group.

6. **One week ahead:** Make sure everyone has a book. Forecast the benefits of studying Jonah, and ask everyone to pray for God's work during the campaign.

7. **The week of the series:** Celebrate and enjoy the wonders of everyone studying and learning together.

8. **During the series:** Collect and share stories of what God is doing in people's lives through the campaign.

9. **After the campaign:** Email me hal@halseedbooks.com to share what you've experienced. Gather a small group of leaders together to evaluate what went well and what might be improved during your next all-church campaign.

Week 1 | Jonah 1

Responding to God's Greatness

Responding to God

"But Jonah ran away from the Lord and
headed for Tarshish."

Jonah 1:2

You'll find Jonah in the section of the Bible called the "Minor Prophets." When I want to find Jonah, I think about a little poem I memorized to navigate this section of the Bible. If you put the first letters of the first five Minor Prophets together, you get "Ho Jo A Oh Jo." (Hosea, Joel, Amos, Obadiah, Jonah.) It's a dopey rhyme, but it gets me there. Once I'm there, I read a story of a man who hears from God.

Jonah opens with, *"The word of the Lord came to Jonah son of Amittai: 'Go to the great city of Nineveh and preach against it, because its wickedness has come up before me'"* (Jonah 1:1-2). So, Jonah goes…the opposite direction. Nineveh is east of Israel; Jonah goes west. He boards a ship sailing for Tarshish, which is in modern-day Spain. You may think Jonah's an idiot for going the wrong way, but on Day 4 you'll see that he had his reasons. (Now might be a good time to begin reading the first chapter of Jonah if you haven't already done so.)

Soon after setting sail, God sends a strong wind. Waves start pounding the ship, and the sailors are terrified. They lose their lunch, and then they lose their cargo. And when sailors are so frightened that they abandon their payload, you can bet there's some serious seas.

At this point in the story, a little comedy sneaks in. Everyone gets religion except Jonah, the prophet. These crusty pagan sea-goers start praying their knuckles white, but Jonah fluffs his pillow and sleeps in the now-empty cargo hold. From a human perspective, it looks like all is lost; fortunately, there is more to this world than the human perspective. Chapter one is a classic example of a "great reversal." All seems to be lost, then an intervention happens, and all is saved. In this case, Jonah gets tossed overboard, and everyone lives happily ever after.

From a cosmic perspective, the hand of God is all over this story. The story begins with a call: *"Go to the great city of Nineveh and preach against it"* (v. 1). God is too *great* to ignore what is going on in Nineveh and too full of *grace* to judge them without warning. Next, God's *greatness* over nature controls the winds and the waves; they move to His purposes. He controls the fish; it follows where He leads it and swallows what He feeds it. He controls fate; when the sailors cast lots, the lot falls to Jonah. Even the sailors are moved by this mighty God as they pray (v. 5). They even offer sacrifices and make sacred vows (v. 16). So Jonah 1 shines a spotlight on a great and grace-filled God. It begins with grace: sending a warning to Nineveh; it ends with grace: the saving of the sailors. In the middle is God's greatness over wind, waves, seas, sailors, lots, fish and prophets.

How Do You Respond to a God Like That?

1. *You can do what He asks.* That's what nature did. The wind, waves and fish all responded by doing exactly what God asked them to do.

2. *You can worship Him.* That's what the sailors did. Right on the deck of the ship, they knelt and made sacrifices to God.

3. *You can change your lifestyle.* The sailors did that, too. They made vows about what they were going to do and how they were going to live once their voyage was over.

4. *You can run the other direction.* That's what Jonah did. He wanted nothing to do with God's plan, so instead of heading east towards Nineveh, he sailed west towards Spain.

What about you? As we begin this study together, take a minute to benchmark your current condition before a great and gracious God. How have you been responding to Him lately? How do you want to respond to Him today? We will take a closer and more personal look at these questions as we journey with Jonah over the next four weeks together.

THE FINE ART OF QUESTION-ASKING

"So they asked him, 'Tell us, who is responsible for making all
this trouble for us? What do you do? Where do you come from?
What is your country? From what people are you?'"

Jonah 1:8

Have you ever noticed that the most engaging people are always
good question-askers? While my wife Lori and I were in graduate
school, we were invited to dinner by Gary and Suzanne Preston—
twice. During the first dinner, we had the time of our lives. Why?
Simply because Gary and Suzanne asked us a thousand questions.
Before our second dinner, Lori suggested, "Let's try to turn the
conversation to them tonight." So we did, or at least we tried. All
night long, one of us would ask a question, and they would answer
briefly, ending with something like, "And what about you?" Once
again, we had the time of our lives. Since then, I've tried to become
good at question-asking myself.

One thing I've discovered: good question-askers ask *lots*
of questions, sort of like the sailors in Jonah 1:8. *"Tell us, who is
responsible for making all this trouble for us? What do you do? Where do
you come from? What is your country? From what people are you?"* Five
questions in one verse; that's got to be some sort of Bible record. I
don't know if these mariners were normally good question-askers. I

suspect they fired so many questions at Jonah because they hoped to learn how to save their own lives. By the end of the chapter, they seem to have done just that. Jonah 1:16 says, *"At this the men greatly feared the Lord, and they offered a sacrifice to the Lord and made vows to him."*

How to Ask Good Questions

Good questions show you're interested in other people, interested in learning, and most importantly not interested in impressing people with how much you know. These three simple steps might help you get started asking good questions:

1. *Try.* Decide that you really want to learn, understand and/or get to know a person.

2. *Once you've made that decision, ask questions to learn more, not to say more.* Often people ask questions as a means to turn the subject to what they want to talk about. Instead of listening to the answer, these types listen for an *opening.* As soon as the other person is done, they jump in. Great question-askers *don't* jump in. They reflect ("Hmmm. I see what you mean."), clarify ("Am I hearing you say…?"), or nod in agreement, encouraging the speaker to continue.

3. *Listen and use more non-verbals.* Good question-askers are always good listeners. Good listeners show their interest with eye contact, facial expression and posture. Around 94% of all communication is non-verbal, so good listeners can sometimes communicate more *without* words than good speakers can communicate *with* words.

What If I'm Not a Good Listener?

Good listening is an attitude. Philippians 2:4 says, *"Each of you should look not only to your own interests, but also to the interests of others."* If you're interested, you'll listen. If you *want* to know, you'll ask. If you ask, you're well on your way to mastering one of the most important skills in getting along with people. In Jonah 1, we find one great listener and a boatload of good question-askers. Look at this dialogue:

Sailors: *"Tell us, who is responsible for making all this trouble?"*

Jonah: No response.

Sailors: *"What do you do?"*

Jonah: No response.

Sailors: *"Where do you come from?"*

Jonah: No response.

Sailors: *"What is your country?"*

Jonah: No response.

Sailors: *"From what people are you?"*

Jonah didn't want to self-disclose. If it was available back then, he would have pled the Fifth Amendment. Since it wasn't, he answered finally, *"I am a Hebrew and I worship the Lord, the God of heaven, who made the sea and the land"* (Jonah 1:9). Good question-askers that they were, the sailors responded with, *"What have you done?"*

Jonah: No response.

Sailors: "What should we do to you to make the sea calm down for us?"

Finally, a response!

Jonah: *"Pick me up and throw me into the sea, and it will become calm. I know that it is my fault that this great storm has come upon you."*

Reluctantly, the sailors do. First, they try rowing back to shore. God's greatness keeps them from making any progress against the waves. Next, they appeal to His grace. *"They cried out to the Lord, 'O Lord, please do not let us die for taking this man's life'"* (Jonah 1:14). They're not only good listeners; they have good hearts. They try everything in their power to keep from harming this irresponsible Hebrew, even though he is the instigator of their distress. At the end of the day, these nameless sailors got more than they asked for: their lives are saved, and their souls seem to have been saved as well.

Picture this scene for a minute. You're a Phoenician sailor. You've picked up cargo and a few passengers, and you're sailing north towards Phoenicia, anticipating a healthy payday. You believe in God; in fact, from your childhood you've been taught that there are *many gods*, one for every river, tree, mountain and ocean. Now you're out on the ocean experiencing a God-sized storm. You do what you know: you and your mates pray to your favorite god and even jettison the cargo, but it doesn't help. You're about to sink, and you know it. What do you do? You ask questions, as many as you can until you find the truth.

One of the passengers claims that his God is the "God of heaven," the Creator God who made the land and the sea. You're not sure that's possible, but minutes from drowning you'll keep asking questions. "Why is God mad at you? What can we do about it?" You're tempted to follow up with, "And why should we believe you?" but there's really no time. At this point, it's either believe or perish.

So you offer a quick prayer to this new almighty God, and you throw His prophet overboard, and the seas calm. You're going to live. You're going to reach land. You're going to embrace your wife again, hold your children again, eat again, sleep again, dream again and hope again. Can you imagine the aftermath of all that just happened?

How Do You Respond to a God Like That?

If you're a Phoenician sailor, you worship your newfound God. You offer Him tangible sacrifices to show your gratitude. You make vows to Him about the quality and direction of your life. That's what honest, well-meaning people have been doing since time immemorial. These men encountered the *greatness* of God in the seas and the *grace* of

God in the calming of the sea. They responded by submitting to Him.

Maybe this is something you'd like to do today. The truth is, though it may not be as obvious, God has been great and gracious in *your* life as well. He's created amazing things for you, and He's created you with an incredible ability to see and feel them. You may be tempted to say, "Why should I believe?" Theoretically, that might be a good question. My simple answer to you today is, "Because He is worthy." Admittedly, this response may not be enough for you; if you have more questions, ask them. He's a big God; He can take it. I've written an entire book *(The God Questions)* to help good question-askers find answers. Jesus said in Mathew 7:7, *"Ask and it will be given to you."* The sailors prove this principle. They asked and subsequently received more than they hoped for. They not only lived; they found the one true, living God. If you keep asking, you will too.

Perhaps you don't need to ask more questions. If you already believe, you may want to respond as the sailors did. Offer some words of worship to this great God today, or offer a tangible sacrifice of your time, talents or treasures. Maybe you can start with a vow of, "Here's what you can expect from me today, Lord." However, what if today is the dawn of your "believing"? Like the sailors, you've asked enough questions and now you're ready to submit. If that's the case, say these words out loud:

"Lord, I believe that you are a great and gracious God. I am submitting my life to you today. Forgive me for the ways I've run from you and the things I've done that hurt others. From this moment onward, I want to be a follower of yours."

That's a life and eternity-changing prayer. If you prayed it today for the first time, you will begin to experience more of God's greatness and grace daily. Mark this day and tell someone about it.

Lori and I haven't seen Gary and Suzanne Preston in years, but I think of them whenever I find a good question-asker. I wonder if they're somehow related to a few ancient Phoenician sailors.

FEAR THAT BUILDS FAITH

*"All the sailors were afraid and each
cried out to his own god."*

Jonah 1:5

I went to see *The Perfect Storm* when it first appeared in movie theatres. Large-action adventure films have a much greater impact when seen on the big screen. If you haven't seen it, *The Perfect Storm* is about a crew of fishermen who get caught in the middle of the Atlantic at the convergence of three storms. The plot is built on rising suspense and rising waves. The sailors embark on a sunny day; they encounter a little rain, then a little more rain, then twenty-foot waves, fifty-foot waves, and finally one hundred-foot waves. By the climax, your heart is pounding and you're leaning as far away from the screen as you can in order to get away from the sheer terror of the sea.

The sailors experienced something like that in Jonah 1. They weigh anchor in Israel, heading for their home port of Phoenicia, just up the coast. Mild weather turns inclement, then nasty, then brutal. As waves batter the sides of the ship, then crash over their gunwales and finally break mast-high, it takes all their courage to keep from panicking.

The physical plot is gripping, but another plotline bleeds through on the spiritual level. Focus on one word in the story and you'll see it: *fear.* It appears four times in the text. First, the sailors are *afraid* of the storm (v. 5). Then they interview Jonah and discover that he *fears* Yahweh, "the God of heaven, who made the sea and the land" (v. 9). This escalates their fear. Verse ten says, *"This terrified them…"* The chapter concludes with, *"At this the men greatly feared the Lord"* (v. 16). If you're reading a modern translation, you might miss this progression. The verbs used by The New International Version are *afraid, worship, terrified and greatly feared*, but they're all the same word in Hebrew: "yare". If you follow the progression, you can see into the psyches of these hearty men of the sea.

As the storm progresses, there is growing fear of Mother Nature. These men are *pagans*, meaning they believe that each facet of nature is ruled by a particular god. Yamm, for instance, was the god of the sea. They start out fearing a "god" (little "g"). Then they hear from Jonah that there is a greater God in the universe, one who not only inhabits nature but created it. The men probably reasoned, "If *this* God is involved in what's causing the storm, we're not just in trouble—we're in *big* trouble!" After all, this is the GREAT God; who can survive before Him? What they experience in the next few hours changes everything for them. They fear this great God.

In an attempt to save His prophet, all hands row for shore. Making no progress, they decide their only choice is to trust the prophet's advice and throw him overboard. Before they do so, they plead to this great God for mercy and understanding. *"O Lord, please do not let us die for taking this man's life. Do not hold us accountable for killing an innocent man, for you, O Lord, have done as you pleased"* (v.14). In prayer, they discover a God they never expected; this great God is also gracious! He gives mercy to those who ask for it!

How Do You Respond to a God Like That?

That day was a day of progressive revelation for the sailors. They woke up believing one thing about the universe and went to bed with a completely revised understanding. They knew first-hand that there is one God in the universe; He creates and controls the wind and the waves, and He listens and loves when people pray. The sailors offered

Him sacrifices because it's what they know to do; they've made sacrifices to pagan deities all their lives. Now they make sacrifices to the One True Living God. And they make vows: "From now on, I'm going to…" "From this day forward, I will never again…" We don't know exactly what they sacrificed or vowed, and it really doesn't matter. What matters is how *you* will respond to this God today. Here are some questions that might help you:

1. Is there a sacrifice you'd like to make today to the One True Living God?

2. How would you complete these sentences: "From now on, I'm going to…" "From this day forward, I will never again…"

3. You can bet one of the first things the sailors did upon arriving home was tell friends and family about their experience with God's greatness and grace. Who would you like to tell about your experiences with God today?

If you don't keep a journal already, this might be a great time to start. Seeing your own answers to these questions in print might inspire you to take action.

How to Harden a Tender Heart

"Pick me up and throw me into the sea," he replied, "and
it will become calm. I know that it is my fault that
this great storm has come upon you."

Jonah 1:12

Proverbs 28:14 provides a great contrast between what we learned
yesterday and what we'll learn today: *"Blessed is the man who always fears
the Lord, but he who hardens his heart falls into trouble."* In chapter one,
"trouble" is Jonah's middle name. He's in capital "T"-trouble with God,
people and nature—both animal (a fish) and mineral (the ocean). Only
the plant world has not turned against him—but it will in chapters
two and four! How did it come to this? How did Jonah develop a hard
heart? More importantly, how can you avoid the same mistake?

Jonah was a prophet, a spokesperson for God. They're a rare
breed. Less than 50 prophets are identified in Israel during the 920
years between the time of Moses (1350 BC) and Malachi (430 BC).
To put that into perspective, America has had 43 presidents in the
220 years between George Washington (1789) and George W. Bush
(2008). Prophets are an elite class chosen for their sensitivity to God,
ability to communicate, and willingness to risk ridicule and harm
for God's sake. Jonah must have been an impressive man, steeped in
wisdom and insight and walking closely with the Lord. No doubt at
some point prior to Jonah 1, he possessed a tender-hearted soul.

We know two things for certain about Jonah. (1) His name means "dove." Many people in the Bible have strong correlations between their name and their personality. (2) His birthplace was Gath Hepher in Northern Israel (2 Kings 14:25). According to legend, Jonah was the son of the widow of Zarephath (1 Kings 17:7-24). He lived during the reign of Jeroboam II (782-753 BC). Jeroboam II was an expansion-minded king who restored some territory that Israel had previously lost to her neighbors.

Does all this really help us understand him? Perhaps, but consider the following and how it might have affected Jonah's feelings:

Jonah lived at a time when the nation of Northern Israel and the nation of Assyria were mortal enemies. The Assyrians were known for their brutality. In the records of Ashurbanipal II (884—859 BC), he describes the way he and his men treated the peoples they conquered.

> *"I besieged and conquered the city… I captured many troops alive. I cut off some of their arms and hands. I cut off others their noses, ears and extremities. I gouged out the eyes of many troops. I made one pile of the living and one of heads. I hung their heads on trees around the city. I flayed as many nobles as had rebelled against me and draped their skins over the pile of corpses… I flayed many, right through my land and draped their skins over the walls. I cut off the heads of their fighters and built therewith a tower before the city. I burnt their adolescent boys and girls."[2]*

Jonah may have witnessed this kind of cruelty. We don't know for sure, but imagine what losing a son or father this way would do to your heart. Bottom line: Jonah *hated* the Ninevites. When God said, "Jonah, I'm going to judge them for their wickedness," Jonah's thought was, "The sooner the better." When God said, "I want you to warn them first," Jonah thought, "Not a chance." This thinking was the first step, an understandable step, away from God. People believe Jonah ran from God because he was afraid of God; nothing could be farther from the truth. Jonah ran from God because Jonah *knew* God. He knew that God is great and gracious. (For proof, skip ahead and read Jonah 4:2.) Jonah ran *because* of God's grace. He didn't want that grace extended to the Ninevites. They didn't deserve it, couldn't merit it and hadn't earned it. If it were possible, Jonah was going to make sure they never received it.

---

[2] http://www.adam.com.au/bstett/BAssyriaVsGod.htm

Since they lived to his east, Jonah ran west. The metaphor in his running is interesting. "He went *down* to Joppa…" (v. 3); he went "*below deck*, where he *lay down*" (v. 4); when the lots were cast, the lot *fell* to Jonah (v. 7). Do you see the direction he's heading? By the middle of chapter two, Jonah will be at the bottom of the ocean.

The Start of a Broken Heart

Even so, I'll bet he never saw it coming. You see, the hardening of a tender heart almost always starts with a justifiable action. Jonah probably was thinking, "These people don't deserve mercy, so I'm not going to give it to them." And it's true; they don't. However, it's not about what you or I or Jonah thinks; it's about God's *grace*. The minute you refuse to let God be who He is, you've got a whole mess of problems on your hands.

First, Jonah makes a decision: "I'm going to disregard God's request." Then, he rationalizes: "My thinking is right." Next, he makes a direction-change: "I'm going to go the opposite direction God wants me to go." This precipitates an altitude-change: down to Joppa, down below deck, lying down…going lower and lower and lower. Before he knows it, this once tender-hearted prophet has an attitude-change: "Pick me up and throw me overboard (v. 12); I don't care." By the end of the book, his outlook is so low, he despairs of life. "*O Lord, take away my life, for it is better for me to die than to live*" (Jonah 4:3). The outcome of a hardened heart is often an inability to imagine joy; you can't believe that good things will come to you if you return to God's faithfulness. When our hearts shrink or calcify, our eyes lose the ability to see the good around us. I know many people whose depression started from their decision. They decided to walk their way instead of God's way.[3]

For whatever reason, Jonah just couldn't bring himself to draw God's line of grace around the Ninevites. So he turned his back on God, just this once, just in this *one* instance. I'm sure Jonah intended to be loyal to God in everything else. I'll bet you know someone who's said that as well, and isn't walking with God today.

---

[3] In fairness, I also know many people whose depression started *not* from a decision, but from a chemical imbalance outside of their control.

To me, the really interesting part is that God *still* used Jonah. In chapter three, we'll discover that God used Jonah to pull off one of the greatest harvest miracles in history as an entire city turned to the Lord. Few of God's spokesmen see that breadth of fruit in a lifetime. Apparently hard-heartedness is not an absolute disqualifier from fruitfulness; it's just an absolute disqualifier from hope, joy and closeness with the Father.

When we first started New Song Community Church, I led a Bible Study for seekers who wanted to know if God was real and trustworthy. One of the men in the group, Dave Allen, struggled with the concept of grace. His boss had been killed in a brutal crime, and the pain he felt for her and her loved ones almost kept him from embracing the love God was extending to him. A few weeks after his boss's death, Dave read a news article about a serial killer who had asked for God's forgiveness days before his execution. This too put Dave in a quandary. "Can God really forgive Ted Bundy after all he's done?" he asked me. The thought of that much grace was almost enough for Dave to decide he didn't want to worship a great *and* gracious God. I gave Dave the only answer I know: "Can God really forgive me after all I've done? And can He really forgive you after all you've done? If you were God, where would you draw the line on forgiveness? What sins would you forgive and not forgive? How much grace would be too much?"

Within a few weeks, Dave asked Christ to forgive him and to lead his life. Today, he and his family are active members in a local church. I heard recently that his son Russell was a contender for the Dick Butkus Trophy, awarded to the best college linebacker of the season.

Here's another real-life example. As I'm writing this, God is extending a great amount of grace to Mike McFadden. Mike, a fireman in his 40's, came home from the hospital last week with a new heart. Not a "Jesus made my heart new" kind of heart, but a *new heart*—a heart transplant. A month ago, Mike's heart failed. He was put on the emergency donor list and given only a few weeks to live. Four days later, he had a new heart. Of the only twelve heart transplants that took place in San Diego County in 2007, Mike received one of them, installed by one of the leading cardiologists in the country. Mike came up to me in church yesterday to thank me for praying for him. Don't you love a story of grace like that?

How Do You Respond to a God Like That?

If you were the McFadden family, how would you be responding to God right now? Maybe that's how we ought to respond to God every day. Psalm 118:24 says, *"This is the day the Lord has made, let us rejoice and be glad in it."* There are plenty of things to worry, complain, pout and protest about. But in the face of a God who can forgive a people like the Ninevites and put breath in the lungs of a fireman, how can you *not* rejoice today?

The real question is: what will that rejoicing look like for you? Will you infect your workplace with a positive attitude? Will you hug your spouse more passionately than yesterday? How about working a little harder on your school project out of gratitude to a God who let you experience life today? You've got a lot of choices of how to respond; just don't choose Jonah's way, okay?

Why Greatness and Grace are So Important

"Then the Lord sent a great wind...
great storm... great fish..."

Jonah 1:4, 12, 17

My dictionary defines *great* as "powerful; influential," and *gracious* as "merciful; compassionate." Why, of all the character traits of God, does Jonah spotlight these two? What makes greatness and grace so important?

When theologians try to describe God, they divide His attributes into two categories: "the *personal* and *impersonal* characteristics of God." Personal traits describe how we relate to others, while impersonal traits cover everything about us that doesn't have to do with relationships. You may be a great negotiator, a poor sport, a good conversationalist or polite schmoozer. Those are personal traits, or better, **interpersonal**, because they express how you relate to people. At the same time, you could be handsome, buff, smart or short. Those traits are impersonal; no people or persons are involved with them.

God's personal traits include love, mercy, kindness, patience, helpfulness, etc. If you summed all of these up, you'd come up with one word: *grace*. God is gracious. The New American Webster Dictionary defines gracious as "generous; magnanimous." When He relates to people, He is amazingly gracious. His impersonal traits include big, strong, intelligent and self-sufficient. (Or, if you want the fifty-cent versions, He is omnipresent, omnipotent, omniscient, and has aseity.) Sum those up, and you have "great." God is great. If it were possible to distill God's character into two words, they would be *great* and *gracious*.

God is Great & Gracious.

You might be thinking, "What difference does this make to me?" It makes *all* the difference. God's greatness means that He can do anything. But if that was God's only characteristic, we'd have to add a warning to Him. *Danger: This one is all-powerful!* The good news is, however, God's *grace* means that He cares. I can pray to a God like that, and I can trust a God like that because He's not only able— He's willing. That's a winning combination. In Jonah 1, God is able to control the seas and willing to respond to the sailors. In chapter two, you'll find Him able to control the fish and willing to rescue Jonah. In chapter three, you'll see His ability to get the attention of an entire city and His willingness to forgive every one of them. In chapter four, He's able to grow a plant and willing to counsel with a sulking prophet.

If you turn to other books of the Bible, you'll discover these same traits. In Daniel 4, God towers over the most powerful man in the empire, a despot named Nebuchadnezzar. In His grace, God warns the king about pride; in His greatness, He humbles him. In His grace (again), He restores the king, who then affirms God's greatness by issuing a proclamation to his entire realm. These Twin Peaks of *greatness* and *grace* are also hallmarks of the life of Jesus. One minute He walks on water, feeds five thousand, calms a storm, transfigures His body (greatness), and another He heals a paralytic, raises a widow's son from the dead, weeps with a father, or requests forgiveness for those who hang Him on a cross (grace).

True Examples of God's Grace

In October 2007, San Diego County experienced the worst disaster in its history. Fires enveloped large sections of East County, Escondido, Fallbrook, Camp Pendleton and more. A few hours after these fires began, two of the "fireballs" in our church sprang into action.

Suzanne Duntley and Edwin Samson offered our building as a shelter for evacuees. What started as San Diego's worst disaster became the best week of ministry in New Song's history. We saw God's greatness in the provisions that poured in. Cots, bedding, blankets, food, water and clothing came from all quarters of our community. We saw God's grace through the actions of the volunteers. New Songers roamed the building, joyfully cleaning bathrooms, humbly praying for those in need, and counseling those who lost homes, all with smiles on their faces. We saw the greatness *and* grace of God as "the Lord added to our number daily those who were being saved." By the time it was all over, we had fed and sheltered over 600 people, saw 92 pray to receive Christ, and started a Spanish-speaking congregation the next weekend for our new Latino brothers and sisters.

During that week, I saw hundreds of people responding to God's greatness and grace through service, prayer and giving. The first were our own church members. One member, Dave Wade, visited every Target and Wal-Mart in our area, buying and donating every air mattress they had in stock. His wife Susan spent ten or more hours a day directing traffic in our front office. One of our college students, Matt Bellamy, slept 19 hours the entire week, preferring to serve while the opportunity was available. One of our high school students, Sydney Darling, created an update board to track each fire's progress, so our guests could stay informed about their homes and situations. When Sydney's neighborhood received the call to prepare to evacuate, she said to me, "It's only ten minutes away. Mom will call if we *really* have to evacuate. I don't want to give up what I'm doing." Roy Vallez walked around the building with the widest smile I've ever seen, all the while saying, "It doesn't get any better than this."

There's a church twenty minutes south of us, Tri-City Church, led by Pastor Jim Harper. Tri-City also responded in a big way. New Song has not yet been able to build a kitchen, but Tri-City owns a portable one. The kitchen is housed in a fifty-foot trailer and comes complete, ready to make almost any type of meal. Hearing about our need, these dear brothers and sisters brought their trailer to our shelter, along with dozens of volunteers who cooked meals for 300 to 700 people morning, noon and night.

There's a church forty-five minutes north of us, Compass Bible Church, pastored by my friend Mike Fabarez. On the morning the fires struck, Mike called my house to see if Lori and I were safe. He offered his own home in case we were threatened by the fire. When he found out about our shelter, he sent his associate pastor to help with counseling, paid for plumbing repairs and mobilized his church to provide 500 dinners for the following evening. The Tri-City people were so passionate about cooking for us; I actually think they were a bit disappointed the next night when they didn't get to prepare the meal!

One of the most moving examples of responding to God's greatness came from our congressman, Darrell Issa. Congressman Issa visited us on Thursday morning the week of fires and asked, "What else do you need?" Upon learning that we had no showers, he made a quick phone call. Rite-Aid had a building with showers just two hundred feet from us. Within four hours, Rite-Aid was sponsoring free showers for our fire victims. The next morning, Congressman Issa's assistant showed up a second time to see if we had everything we needed. As she left, she handed me a personal check from Congressman Issa's family. "This is to help with your costs," she said. Without embarrassing our congressman, I will tell you it was not a small check. I saw a similar response from the credit union that holds the mortgage on our building. As the fires began, ECCU[4] decided to help those who were helping fire victims. After hearing our story, CEO Mark Holbrook authorized his staff to deposit $10,000 into our account.

Our Youth Pastor, Jim Britts, studied what was going on in our building and came to a conclusion: "We have plenty of volunteers, but everyone is so busy that no one is praying." So Jim spent *hours* in the prayer room that week, praying about the fires, praying for the fire victims and praying for fruitfulness for Christ.

---

[4] Evangelical Christian Credit Union, Anaheaim, CA.

How Do You Respond to a God Like That?

What's the right way to respond to God's greatness and grace? In the way that fits *you*. Ideally at some point you'll pray like Jim, give like Mark Holbrook and Darrell Issa, and serve like Susan, Matt and Sydney. Most likely, there will be one or two predominant ways you *like* to respond, and that's really the key. *How do you **want** to respond to God? What would make **you** feel good?* Most of the time, whatever you feel like doing will be the very thing that brings the most joy to the Father's heart—and the most satisfaction to yours. Take that step and begin!

Week 2 | Jonah 2

Responding to God's Correction

RESPONDING TO GOD'S CORRECTION

"In my distress I called to the Lord, and he answered me."

Jonah 2:2

In chapter one, Jonah responded to God's greatness. The size of the God-generated waves was too much to ignore. In chapter two, Jonah learns to respond to God's correction. It's a lesson he'll need to master if the Lord is going to use him. And does God use Him? Just wait until you read Jonah 3; you'll read what might be the greatest evangelistic movement of God in all of history.

As you read through the story of Jonah's correction, it will seem familiar to you. It's the normal pattern God uses to correct those He loves. The pattern starts with disobedience, which initiates discipline. This in turn causes distress and usually results in a decision to obey, which then leads to deliverance. I'm almost certain you'll be able to relate to it. Hebrew 12:6 points out that *"The Lord disciplines those he loves."* Discipline is a recurring aspect of the spiritual life. If you've ever been disciplined from on high, it's because God loves you.

DISOBEDIENCE

In Jonah 1:2, God issues a direct command to the prophet: *"Go to the great city of Nineveh and preach against it because its wickedness has come up before me."* This is not a suggestion or request. It's an order; like a father saying to his son, "Jason, it's time to take out the trash." The command from God includes the *what* ("preach"), the *where* ("Nineveh"), the *when* ("go [now]") and the *why* ("because of its wickedness"). This is not the first time Jonah has heard the voice of God. He recognizes it as authentic and authoritative, and he understands what's being asked of him. Jonah feels the full intensity of God's resolve on the issue, but without reply, he pivots on his heels and runs. Bold move, Jonah!

The unwilling prophet is thinking, "The Lord is not going to budge on this one, so there's no point in arguing. But under no circumstances am I going to preach to the Ninevites. Since I can't reason with the Almighty, I might as well put as much distance between us as I can before He realizes I'm digging my heels in." What Jonah hadn't factored into the equation was God's greatness. The eye of the Lord is clear enough to see to Joppa and beyond. His arm is long enough to reach far into the sea. Jonah runs, but he doesn't get far before God begins the inevitable work that every parent must initiate when their child disobeys. God begins the discipline process.

DISCIPLINE

When one of my children needed correction, we would sit down and talk about what they'd done wrong and why their behavior needed to be modified. The conversation was always theoretical. "Suppose you continue to do this. Here's what could happen to you..." "If you choose this course of behavior for your life, here's what it leads to..." As a human father, I didn't have visual aids or the ability to create three-dimensional portraits of what I was trying to illustrate. In chapter two, Jonah learns that God has neither of those limitations.

God, like all good parents, disciplines with love and logic. In Jonah 1:4-17, God employs several visual aids. First, He extends His hand to bring Jonah home. Home is the best place to carry out discipline. If home is too far away, someplace private is the next best thing. Can you think of anywhere more private than the digestive tract of a large fish? God's thinking must have gone something like this. "What I've asked of Jonah is challenging but reasonable, so I'm going to expect full compliance. I've got to stop Him from running and help him do the right thing." This great God has power over the wind and waves, so He uses both to bring His wayward prophet home. And while disciplining Jonah, He demonstrates His power to the sailors in such a compelling way that they turn and worship Him. God is the consummate multi-tasker.

When our children were little, our discipline pattern followed a careful script. When Bryan or Amy's behavior reached a certain magnitude of disobedience, they were sent to their room and given a few minutes to calm down and think about their actions. Then I would join them carrying a wooden kitchen spoon. My goal would be to apply loving discipline in order to help them learn self-discipline.

We would talk about what had gone wrong and how to make it better. Our conversations would be something like this: "Honey, do you understand what you did? Let's talk about how you might be able to do that differently next time. My job is to help you grow up respecting things, and I love you too much not to take my job seriously." When the conversation went well, I didn't need to use the spoon. If there was a belligerent spirit, the spoon brought necessary correction. I applied it to the fanny with a slap that would only sting, never damage or bruise. The point was not to hurt but to help. Sometimes a tiny swat did the trick. Occasionally a second and third were necessary. There would be tears, which always led to tender discussions, hugs and a prayer together. All of our discipline was personal. We never asked (nor allowed) others to do it for us.

In the same way, all of God's discipline is personal. It was God who brought the seas against Jonah, and God summoned and opened the fish's mouth. Jonah gets this. In Jonah 2:3 he credits God, not the sailors, with casting him into the water. In our spanking, we used a spoon, never a hand, because the books we read cautioned about a child's associating pain with his or her parent's hand. God does something similar: instead of *directly disciplining* Jonah, He creatively uses a fish. When our kids got a little older, we used confinement to their rooms as a means of correction. God uses confinement in this case as well.

Isaiah 55:8 says that His ways are not our ways. Please note however, *some* of His ways are like our ways, like the way He disciplines His children. My children are grown now. They've turned out better than I hoped. Most of the credit goes to God, but I think at least *some* of the credit goes to the way they were disciplined. Thinking of and following through with the spanking process was painful for me. It was the right thing to do, but I never enjoyed it.

Like most parents, I would think, "This is going to hurt me a lot more than it hurts you." It always did.

God never enjoys disciplining His children. No healthy parent can feel good about causing any sort of pain to their offspring. We discipline because we love our kids too much to let them develop patterns that will harm them later in life. God doesn't need us to feel sorry for Him, but think for a minute about all the uncomfortable situations He must face every day on this planet because of His love for His wayward children.

DISTRESS

A change of attitude is the major purpose of discipline, and inside the fish's belly Jonah's attitude begins to change. The waterlogged prophet says, *"In my distress I called to the Lord, and he answered me"* (Jonah 2:1). Sometimes when I sent the kids to their rooms for a cooling-off period, I would hear, "Daaaad, can you come in so we can talk?" When a child is ready to talk, positive learning can begin. Jonah spends eight verses (2:1-8) describing this phase of his discipline. He's sinking; he's drowning. He's in trouble, and he knows it. So what did he do? He "called to the Lord." Notice how Jonah's attitude has changed here. In chapter one, everyone prays except Jonah. Jonah's heart is too hard. In chapter two, every *word* is a prayer. God has his son's attention, and he wants to talk again. That's what happens in most successful child-discipline situations.

DECISION TO OBEY

After talking awhile (vv. 1-8), Jonah says, *"I… will sacrifice to you. What I have vowed I will make good"* (v. 9). You know things are back to normal when your son or daughter wants to do what you ask. His or her heart is soft again. When my children reached this stage, we would usually develop a game plan for what to do if this situation came up again. I believe that's what God and Jonah did between verses nine and ten. Jonah said, *"What I have vowed, I will make good,"* and the Lord said, *"And I'll help you with it."* Once the game plan was settled, *"The Lord commanded the fish, and it vomited Jonah onto dry land"* (v. 10).

DELIVERANCE

The final step in Jonah's discipline process was *deliverance*. In the language of child-discipline, he's "let out of his bedroom" and allowed to return to normal life. Jonah's final words before being expunged from the fish were, *"Salvation comes from the Lord"* (v. 9). *Deliverance* is another word for salvation, and vice versa. Chapter one ends with a picture of God's greatness: He summons a fish to discipline Jonah. Chapter two ends with a picture of God's grace: He summons the fish to restore Jonah to land.

HOW DO YOU RESPOND TO A GOD LIKE THAT?

If you're like me, you'd like to apologize for the things you've done that have hurt Him. I want to be a joy to my Father, not a nuisance, problem or troublemaker. In fact, after I finish typing this, I think I'll spend a few minutes talking through some things I may be doing that are troubling, disobedient or rebellious toward Him. You may want to do the same. Here's what I'm going to pray: "I'm sorry, Father, for the pain I've caused you recently. I know it's no fun watching me behave this way, and I know you don't enjoy correcting me. Thank you for Your discipline. Like Jonah, I want to say, *'What I have vowed, I will make good'* (v. 9). Oh, and thanks for not using the fish on me."

Praying Through Your Circumstances

"You hurled me into the deep, into the very heart
of the seas, and the currents swirled about me; all your
waves and breakers swept over me."

Jonah 2:3

In 1985, Lori and I volunteered for the mission field. Our destination
was Brazil. Our first task was support-raising, which took eighteen
months. While making plans to ship all of our worldly goods to
South America, we were bombarded by second thoughts. For three-
and-a-half years we'd been trying to have children. Specialists told
us, "Frankly, if you move to Brazil, you'll never have children." For
weeks we struggled with Jesus' words in Matthew 10:37: *"Anyone who
loves his father or mother more than me is not worthy of me; anyone who
loves his son or daughter more than me is not worthy of me."* We knew
two things: first, we had what we believed was a God-given desire
to have children. Second, Brazilians believe that children are a sign
of blessing; a childless couple would not make a great impression on
them. We counseled with parents, pastors and missions executives.
Some said, "Go anyway." Others said, "You should stay home."
God's opinion was the most important to us, so we spent a lot of time
praying. Increasingly, we felt the Lord saying, "I have other plans for
you." To make sure, we set aside an entire day, drove to a secluded
park and spent the day in prayer.

Spending so much time in prayer can seem like a daunting task.
How do you pray for eight to ten hours straight? Actually, once you
get started, it's surprising how quickly the time passes, but more
surprising was what happened inside of us. The day in the park gave
us a sense of peace that's hard to describe. Imagine how awkward
and embarrassed you would feel if you told everyone you know that

you were going to spend the rest of your life in a foreign country, and then you had to come back and tell them you'd changed your mind. People who complete less than a full four years on the mission field are called "first-term casualties," not an easy stigma to live with. Not only were we not going to complete four years in Brazil, we weren't even going to get on a plane. Still, we found peace through prayer!

Lori and I drove home from our prayer day with a peace-filled confidence that the Lord wanted us to pursue the call He had originally given me thirteen years earlier. When I was 15 years old, I had a distinct sense that God wanted me to serve in a local church. Since that day in 1985, I have taken scores of prayer days. I try to schedule at least four per year. They are good for me and for every person I touch, because I come home a better, more passionate, focused and well-intentioned leader. Every time I invest extended time in prayer, I experience the promise of James 4:8 (NASB), *"Draw near to God and he will draw near to you."* Our day at the park not only clarified our career; we came home feeling closer to the Father. We felt His presence, and that presence stayed close for many days. Exodus 34 reports whenever Moses met with God, His face glowed for days.[5] Ours got slightly sunburned. The "glow" for us was the tangible sense of God's nearness.

> Philippians 4:6-7 says,
>
> *"Present your requests to God. And the peace of God will guard your hearts…"*

What was happening inside of the fish in Jonah 2 was pretty much like what happened inside Lori and me during our day at the park. Jonah was praying through his circumstances. He was nearly dead when the fish rescued him. *"The engulfing waters threatened me, the deep surrounded me; seaweed was wrapped around my head. …My life was ebbing away…"* (v. 5, 7). At best, he was dazed; at worst, he may have been slipping into unconsciousness. It's possible that when he woke up inside the fish, he didn't know exactly where he was. In verse two he says, *"From the depths of the grave* [in Hebrew the word is "Sheol," which is the place of the dead] *I called for help."* For a brief moment, he may have thought he'd died and gone to hell.

---

[5] 2 Corinthians 3:13 explains that Moses wore a veil after those meetings, because he didn't want the people to see that the glow was fading.

The Fish Prayer

What would you do if you were locked in a watery grave? My guess is you'd pray your knuckles white. Jonah's fish-prayer followed a pattern that troubled saints have found helpful for ages. Let's take a look at that pattern:

1. Jonah begins by recounting what happened to him (vs. 1-7), then makes a request. *"...my prayer rose to you..."* (v. 7b).

2. With a growing sense of peace, he expresses faith in the Lord. *"I will sacrifice to you..."* (v. 9a).

3. Next, Jonah commits to doing God's will. *"I will make good on my vow..."* (v. 9b).

4. Ultimately, he closes with a word of praise. *"Salvation comes from the Lord"* (v. 9c).

The next time you need God's guidance, you might find Jonah's pattern helpful, and here's an easy way to remember it: **FAITH**

Feelings—Express your thoughts and feelings about your circumstances.

Affirmation—Affirm that God is big enough to handle them and that you trust Him.

Intentions—State your intention, in faith, to follow wherever He leads.

Thanks—Thank Him for what He's done in the past.

Hope—Choose to believe that He will come through again.

I follow this pattern often. Somewhere in the midst of the process, I either get a sense of clarity on what He wants me to do next, or a sense of peace that He's with me, even though the circumstance might stay messy for awhile.

Jesus prayed the first part of this pattern when He was in the Garden of Gethsemane. *"My soul is overwhelmed with sorrow..."* (Feelings, Matthew 26:37). *"My Father..."* (Affirmation, v. 39a). *"Not as I will, but as you will..."* (Intentions, v. 39b). At this point the pattern changes, because it is Jesus who needs to be thanked. Instead of needing hope, Jesus was (and is) the hope of the world. In Psalm 17:6, David sums up the reason people pray: *"I call on you, O God, for you will answer me..."* We pray because God listens and responds.

How Do You Respond to a God Like That?

Give the FAITH pattern a try. What circumstance are you facing that needs God's input or guidance? Take a blank sheet of paper and write a prayer to God using these headings:

1. Lord, these are my feelings right now....

2. I affirm my faith in You because…

3. My intention is to…

4. Thank you for…

5. My hope now is…

Listen for God to speak to you while you are writing. You might find that you get through the entire outline and still haven't sensed His presence. If that's the case, wait quietly for a few minutes. Psalm 46:10 says, *"Be still and know that I am God."* Wait for Him. Peace doesn't usually come while you're moving 90 miles an hour. Slow your heart rate and talk to Him—or just listen. If He can speak to Jonah in the belly of the fish, He can speak to you right where you are. When He does, write down what you think He said or how it made you feel. If you'd like to share it with someone, email me at hal@halseedbooks.com.

ENQUIRING MINDS WANT TO KNOW...

"You brought my life up from the pit, O Lord my God."

Jonah 2:6

Like most good books, Jonah raises almost as many questions as it answers. I wonder if these made your top ten list:

1. After Jonah was thrown overboard, how long did it take the raging sea to calm down?

2. How long was Jonah in the water before he was swallowed by the fish?

3. How far from shore was he when the fish scooped him up?

4. Was Jonah conscious or unconscious at the time of swallowing?

5. Could someone actually survive in a fish's stomach for three days?

6. How badly did the gastric juices sting, and how much of Jonah was digested by the time he was vomited up?

7. What did Jonah look like when he reached shore?

8. What motivated Jonah to write his story? After all, it doesn't paint him in a very flattering light.

9. The prayer Jonah recorded: did he memorize it, or did he re-create it *mostly* from memory when he was finally in a place where he could write it down?

10. When Jonah ran, why did God give him a second chance? Why didn't He choose someone else?

After days of study, I can only conjecture and guess. (You might find it interesting to spend a few minutes thinking about the answers and perhaps begin some clue-searching for yourself.) On the other hand, there are some things I do know about this story:

1. Jonah did not make it to Nineveh inside the fish. Check a map. For the fish to get to Nineveh, it would have had to swim westward the full length of the Mediterranean Sea, then south and circumnavigate all of Africa, then northeastward to and through the entire Persian Gulf, and finally up most of the Tigris River. That's approximately 14,000 miles. Granting it a full 72 hours, this aquarian marvel would have to average 200 miles an hour.

2. One of the gods worshiped by the Phoenicians was the fish god *Yamm*. If Jonah's fish deposited him anywhere near Phoenicia (just north of Israel on the eastern Mediterranean coast), this event would have made quite an impression on all Phoenician Yamm-worshipers—one that might have reverberated all the way to Nineveh. I suppose this might explain why the Ninevites were so receptive to Jonah's message—or not. That's another one of those unanswered questions.

3. Nineveh is about 700 miles from Phoenicia. Jonah had a long walk and a long time to recover from any injuries he experienced from the fish-incident. If for instance his eyebrows, hair and outer layer of skin had been digested, they would have grown back by the time he reached the city. However, if chunks of flesh deeper than the epidermis were digested, well, that's another story.

4. Jonah's rescue by a fish is a miracle. A miracle, by definition, is something beyond the laws of nature. Since God invented the laws of nature, miracles are just recreational activity for Him. R.K. Harrison[6] has documented cases where people have been swallowed by fish or whales and survived. But this one not only swallowed Jonah; it deliberately deposited him on dry land.

5. Jonah's fish-miracle was a *rescue* miracle. The Ninevites' repentance was also a rescue miracle. The prophet was saved from death; the Ninevites were saved from the judgment of God, as well as impending death.

---

[6] Harrison, R.K.: *Introduction to the Old Testament; with a Comprehensive Review of Old Testament Studies and a Special Supplement on the Apocryphia.* Grand Rapids, MI: Eerdmans, June 1969. Pages 908-909.

6. Jonah's miracle would not have been necessary if he had obeyed the first time.

7. When God spoke to Jonah, Jonah ran the opposite direction. When God spoke to the fish, the fish swam to precisely where God wanted him. Sometimes fish are more faithful than prophets.

8. God used this miracle to forecast the miracle of the resurrection of His Son (Matthew 12:40).

9. In the minds of ancient Middle Easterners, the nation of Israel was associated with the constellation Pisces (the fish). This fish-miracle may have contributed to the association. Numbers 24:17 says *"a star will rise out of Jacob."* The star that guided the Wise Men may have been some sort of stellar phenomenon going on in the constellation Pisces, which is how they knew the King was born in Israel (Matthew 2:2).

10. God's *greatness* in breeding, directing and providing the amazing fish at just the right moment, and His *grace* in using it to rescue Jonah from the sea, are both displayed in this one miracle.

How Do You Respond to a God Like That?

One way to respond to a God like this is to watch for Him. His greatness is reflected in everything He has made, including people. Until I read the book of Jonah, I didn't think about God's greatness and grace very often; now I'm seeing these qualities everywhere. For instance, my office window at home looks out on some amazing foothills. They change hue as the sun rises behind them, shines above them, and then descends to the west. At every hour they exude greatness.

And grace abounds. Last night I attended the wedding of Edwin and Amy Samson. Edwin is a member of New Song Church's staff. His life is a daily unfolding of grace. As a young Navy corpsman, God's grace preserved him during Operation Iraqi Freedom. He returned home and found Christ in our church—another example of grace. Not long after, his first wife left him. While working at night as a custodian, he completed his bachelor's degree. Now he's excelling in seminary, just a few semesters away from a master's degree. Last night was one big great-grace moment as 400 New Songers witnessed Edwin's union to an outstanding young woman with a heart and zeal equal to his own.

God's grace flows daily in sustaining, providing, forgiving, restoring, infusing hope, giving second chances... the list is endless. Look for it today and you'll see what I mean.

OPEN HANDS

"Those who cling to worthless idols forfeit the
grace that could be theirs."

Jonah 2:8

You may have heard of a study taught in most first-year psychology classes about a monkey reaching his hand through the bars of his cage to get a peanut. The bars are just wide enough for the monkey to get his hand through, but just narrow enough to keep him from bringing his fist back inside when it's wrapped around the peanut. The result: the hapless monkey sits there clutching the peanut. He'd rather be immobilized with his prize than free without it. I imagine that scene when I read the eighth verse of Jonah's prayer: *"Those who cling to worthless idols forfeit the grace that could be theirs."* Picture a creature clinging to a worthless stone; only it's not a monkey, it's a human. Maybe it's you or me.

I have discovered that many of life's turning points are triggered by flashes of insight. I call them *"Aha!-Moments."* One of my first *Aha!-Moments* came when I realized I could swim faster than most of my friends—and I enjoyed it. That moment motivated me to spend much of my childhood in the water. One of my most important *Aha!-Moments* came when I realized that I wanted to spend the rest of my life with Lori Hammer. That moment motivated me to "pop the question."

Jonah experiences an *Aha!-Moment* while camping inside the great fish. Upon first swallow, the prophet was near panic. Thinking he might actually be dead[7], he did what most of us would do in a similar situation: he cried out to God. Prayer has a calming effect[8], so before long Jonah

[7]2:2, *"From the depths of the grave I called for help."* "Grave" is the Hebrew word, "Sheol", the place of the dead.

[8]Philippians 4:6-7, *"Do no be anxious about anything, but in everything... present your requests to God. And the peace of God... will guard your hearts and your minds in Christ Jesus."*

was able to slow down his heart rate and think rationally about his situation. That's when his *Aha!* came. Suddenly it dawned on him that he was better off inside the fish than most people are outside the fish. "It's better to be fish food," he reasoned, "than to live outside of a relationship with God." His exact words were *"Those who cling to worthless idols forfeit the grace that could be theirs."*

JONAH'S MUSING

Here's what I picture happening: As Jonah is thrown off the ship, his brain is imprinting the looks on the sailors' faces. They're terrified, coupled with a twinge of hope. They're wondering if Yahweh is really the God behind the storm, and if so, will He be gracious to them once they've jettisoned His servant? Inside the fish, Jonah thinks about these faces. Phoenicians worshiped a family of deities. El was the head of the gods with his wife/consort Asherah. Adonis was a young, handsome god. Mot was the god of death; Yamm, the god of the sea; Yarih, the god of the moon; and Shapsh, the god of the sun. None of them were gracious or compassionate. What if this Yahweh, whom Jonah claimed was the Creator God, really was different?

As soon as Jonah hit the water, the sea began to calm down. That's when the sailors responded to God with vows and sacrifices. I don't know whether Jonah could still see these men after he landed in the water. I suspect the raging sea distanced him from the boat too quickly for him to get a glimpse of their Yahweh worship. I imagine that during his fish-belly musings, he thought about them again. "Were they still clinging to Yamm and Mot, like the monkey behind the bars, or did they recognize the greatness of the One True Living God and choose to let go and follow Him?" Then it hit him: "*I* know the One True Living God personally! I have a relationship with Him. He's been gracious to me! I am better off inside this fish *with* God's love than people who aren't in fish-bellies but worship idols made of stone."

I have never worshiped a stone image in my life, and I imagine you haven't either. Most of the images we worship are far subtler: the American Dream, achieving a coveted position at work, earning a certain annual figure, or even owning a particular car, truck, boat, plane, four-wheeler, etc. These are the things Americans live for, or at least trade large blocks of their time for. An honest way to measure what, or who, you're living for is to look at your calendar and in your wallet. Where are you spending the bulk of your time and treasure? Those may be your idols.

Notice two words in Jonah's musings: *"Those who cling to worthless idols forfeit the grace that could be theirs."* One is "cling." Once the monkey grasps the nut, he's caught. Unable to get the nut and unwilling to let go of it, he *clings* to it, rejecting all rationality. The other word is "grace." The New Testament word for grace is *charis*; it means "unmerited favor." This is the Old Testament word *hesed*. It's used 248 times in the Bible. Usually it's translated "unfailing love", "steadfast love" or "kindness". *Hesed* is God's *loyal love.* He loved the nation of Israel because of their relationship with Him, in spite of all the times they turned their back on Him. *Hesed* is God's fierce love for His children, and it's available to anyone who will follow Him. God commissioned Jonah, directed him to the Ninevites, whipped up the storm, summoned the fish, and calmed the sea, all because of His *hesed*. This great God, because of His *hesed*, cared enough about the Ninevites to send them a prophet, enough about the sailors to save their lives, and enough about Jonah to restore him and give him a second chance.

How Do You Respond to a God Like That?

Imagine yourself with your hands through the bars. They're grasping something material or ethereal, something less than God, but something you deeply desire. Would it be worth it to release your grip and reach out that now-free hand to the One True Living God?

Sometimes when I'm praying, I will open both my hands and say, "Lord, whatever you'd like to put into my hands, they're open to you." The key is to *open your hands*. Have you ever opened your hands to God? Have you ever said, "Lord, I'm yours; everything I am and all I have are yours."? If not, your perfect response today is to open your hands and invite Him in. Pray something like this: *"Lord, come into my life today. Forgive me for the things I've clung to in the past and the things I've done that I shouldn't have. Lead me from now on. Put into my hands whatever you'd like. I'm yours."* If you prayed that prayer, I'd like to give you some tools to help you in your new relationship with God. You can reach me at hal@halseedbooks.com.

Another possibility is that you've already given your life to Christ, but you've stuck your hands back through the bars and taken hold of something that's now taken hold of you. Your response to a great and gracious God ought to include releasing the thing to which you now cling. You might want to pray: *"Lord, I have been clinging to_____*

_____ and shouldn't be. I now release him/ her/it to you. Lead me once again."

Talking about being part of a local church, Paul says, *"Cling to what is good. Be devoted to one another in brotherly love. Honor one another above yourselves"* (Romans 12:9b). If you're not part of a small group or team in your local church, another valid response would be to join a group this week and begin building some close, God-honoring friendships. It's much easier to keep from grabbing onto things you shouldn't when you're living life alongside other people who are trying to keep from grabbing things too.

What's on Your Mind?

*"In my distress I called to the Lord, and he answered me.
From the depths of the grave I called for help and
you listened to my cry."*

Jonah 2:2

Scott Campbell gets the credit for opening my eyes to a new dimension of spirituality. The Campbell's lived two doors from us many years ago. We bumped into each other a lot and eventually became friends. Scott has a deep faith in Christ, so one day I asked him if he'd like to get together to pray once a week. His response was, "I'll pray with you, if you memorize Scripture with me." I didn't really think I could memorize Scripture. I certainly never thought I'd enjoy it, but Scott was an excellent tutor. He'd been trained by the Navigators while in college and knew exactly what to do to absorb Scripture into the brain. The first week we met, I got so motivated that I memorized nine verses. After that, I settled down to a more realistic pace: one or two verses a week. At last count, I had memorized over 1,300 verses.

Interestingly, I discovered that memorizing Scripture increased my memory for other things. Our brains are like the other muscles in our bodies: the more we use them, the more they adapt and become useful. Better memory is only one benefit, though. Americans are exposed to approximately 5,000 advertisements every day, five thousand messages that say, "In order for you to be fulfilled, to have satisfaction, to achieve success, you must buy me, try me, taste me, wear me, and put me in your hair." Without trying very hard, I'll bet you can access a half-dozen of those messages in your mind right now, with music accompanying each of them. Carrying Scripture in my mind helps undo the effects of those messages. It rebalances my thoughts on what is true, right, profitable and worth spending my time and energy on.

Hide His Word In Your Heart!

Not only has the Scripture in my memory bank renewed my mind, it has helped me ward off temptation. One of the first verses I memorized with Scott was Psalm 119:9, 11: *"How can a young man keep his way pure? By living according to your Word…I have hidden your word in my heart that I might not sin against you."* More than once, the Holy Spirit has been able to steer me away from a cheap thrill, lazy indulgence or careless action by whispering Scripture in my ear. This is another benefit I've discovered from Scripture memory: having a repository of truth embedded in my head allows the Holy Spirit to counsel me when I need counsel, direct me when I need direction, encourage me when I need courage and correct me when I need correcting. Scripture memory is like my iPod: I download songs into it, and then when I want to hear that certain song, I select it from my playlist. When the Holy Spirit wants to communicate with me, He almost always accesses the playlist of Scriptures I've downloaded into my mind. He dials up the verse, it plays automatically and I say, "Ah! That's just what I needed!"

That's not all. I have three academic degrees in Bible and related subjects; none of them have enabled me to think through Scripture the way memorizing it has. Whenever I memorize a verse, I start by reading the paragraphs before and after the one that contains my verse so I'm aware of the context. As a result, wherever I have a verse memorized, I have a fairly good idea of what's taking place in the section surrounding it. My mind can think through dozens of books of the Bible, chapter by chapter, because I've got a verse or two memorized in each of those chapters. It's like carrying an index with me. I can't tell you how helpful that has been, not only to me personally, but to people who ask my advice or counsel.

One more thing: Scripture memory has increased my love for the Bible. Jeremiah says, *"When your words came, I ate them; they were my joy and my heart's delight"* (Jeremiah 15:16). Whenever I memorize a verse of Scripture, I feel like I've chewed and swallowed it, and it has become part of me. I love the Bible, in part, because I *know* the Bible. I have absorbed it into my bones. King David must have had a similar experience, because in Psalm 19:10 he says that God's words *"… are sweeter than honey…"* to him.

I am confident that Jonah memorized large portions of Scripture. Dissect his prayer, and it becomes obvious. For instance, Jonah 2:2-3 says: *"In my distress I called to the Lord and he answered me. From the deaths of the grave I called for help, and you listened to my cry. You hurled me into the deep, into the very heart of the seas, and the currents swirled about me; all your waves and breakers swept over me."*

Look at this:

"In my distress, I called to the Lord…" Psalm 18:6

"…you have delivered me from the depths of the grave." Psalm 86:13

"You have put me in the lowest pit, in the darkest depths." Psalm 88:6

"…all your waves and breakers have swept over me." Psalm 42:7

If you compare the actual Hebrew version in Jonah with the Psalms referenced, you would see a close resemblance.[9] Jonah is praying Scripture, line after line! No doubt this is part of the reason God called Jonah; he knew the Scriptures so well, he could quote them while crammed inside a fish's belly. His memorized Scriptures sustained him, gave him hope and kept his mind occupied and fruitful during three very harrowing days. It can do the same for you.

How Do You Respond to a Challenge Like This?

I hope you'll consider adopting the habit of Scripture memory. At least give it a try by memorizing one verse a week for the next month. I have a few suggestions to get you off to a good start:

[9] H.L. Ellison: *The Expositor's Bible Commentary*, Vol. 7, p. 364, developed this chart to illustrate the number of "quotations or reminiscences" Jonah uses from the Psalms: Jonah Psalms
2:21 3:4, 120:1
2:2b 18:4-5; 30:3
2:3a 88:6-7
2:3b 42:7
2:4a 31:22
2:4b 5:7
2:5a 69:1-2
2:6b 29:15; 56:13; 103:4
2:7a 107:5; 142:3
2:8a 31:6

1. **Give yourself some motivation.**
   Here are six verses that declare how important God's Word is. Choose one and begin memorizing it today: Matthew 4:4; 2 Timothy 3:16-17; Psalm 119:105; Deuteronomy 32:46-47; Proverbs 30:5, Psalm 19:7.

2. **Get the context.**
   Before memorizing, read the paragraphs before and after the verse. This will help you understand what the verse is really saying. It will also help you to remember the general subject of the whole passage for the rest of your life.

3. **Pick a title.**
   To help with recall later, create a short title for the verse. Write your title on the top of a 3x5 or flash card; you'll carry it with you as your memory card. For instance, if you're memorizing one of the motivational verses above, a good title might be *God's Word*.

4. **Memorize one phrase at a time.**
   If you're memorizing Psalm 119:105, start with, *"Your word is a lamp to my feet."* Nail that down before moving on to *"and a light to my path."*

5. **Involve as many senses as possible.**
   Memorizing is a skill that will improve as you use it. Start by using as many of your senses as you can, all at the same time. Write the verse clearly and carefully on your memory card. Then get a piece of scratch paper and write the phrase over and over again while saying it out loud. This will involve sight, hearing, and touch—and increase your retention.

6. **Get the words perfect.**
   Make sure you memorize the words perfectly. This is Scripture; hold it sacred. If you memorize it wrong the first time, it will be hard to get the wrong words out of your mind.

7. **Say the reference twice.**
   The reference is important in order to know where the verse is located. This will be the hardest part to retain, so always write

2:9a 50:14; 69:30; 107:22
2:9c 3:8; 37:39

and say it at both the beginning and end of the verse. Example:

God's Word
Psalm 119:105
Your word is a lamp to my feet and a light to my path.
Psalm 119:105

8. **Review the verse every day for eight weeks.**
    Say the verse out loud perfectly, and picture it in your mind as you do. After eight weeks it will be embedded in your long term memory, and you will "own" the verse. Write the date on the card that you begin memorizing, and you'll know when the eight weeks are up. Each day recite the verse from memory, then read the verse from your memory card to see that you've got the words perfectly. Practice does not make perfect, it makes *permanent*. Get it perfect *before* you get it permanent.

9. **Get a partner.**
    Scott Campbell and I checked each other on our newly-memorized verses every week for two years. We set a specific time, handed each other our new cards, and then took turns listening and checking for accuracy. Meeting regularly with Scott held me accountable to my commitment of memorizing one or two verses every week. Knowing that an inspection was coming, I worked harder to have those verses down pat before our meeting.

10. **Review the verse monthly for a year.**
    Once you've recited the verse for eight weeks, file it. Once a month, pull your old cards out and review each of them to make sure you've still got them word-perfect. I should warn you, though: once you start this process, you'll find yourself becoming addicted to it! You'll also discover that the benefits far outweigh the time and brainpower spent.

After memorizing my favorite passages and many verses suggested by others, I decided to memorize the key verse for each book of the Bible. In case you're interested in doing the same, I've reconstructed the list for you on the last page of this book.

Week 3 | Jonah 3

RESPONDING TO GOD'S GRACE

Responding to God's Grace

"Then the word of the Lord came to Jonah
a second time... Jonah obeyed the word
of the Lord and went to Nineveh."

Jonah 3:2-3

From time to time, a well-meaning Bible-reader will ask me, "Why is it that God is such an angry God in the Old Testament and such a loving God in the New Testament? It's like there are two different Gods." When I hear this question, two thoughts fire up simultaneously: one is "I'm glad you're reading enough to make this observation!" and the other is "I'm sorry you're missing the details." What happens in Jonah 3 is as clear an example of the loving nature of God as found anywhere in the Bible. Jonah 1 and 2 showcase the greatness of God as He dominates men and nature. Chapters three and four settle on the graciousness of God as He gives second chances to an undeserving prophet and an unworthy nation.

In chapter two, Jonah's discipline process concludes with his decision to obey. It resumes in chapter three as one decision results in many decisions—hundreds of thousands of them. Jonah goes to the metropolis of Nineveh, walks one day's march into the city, and shouts, *"Forty more days and Nineveh will be overturned"* (v. 4). No exclamation point, no extrapolation, no details. Jonah may have said more than that, though the text gives the impression he left it at just that. After all, Jonah didn't really want these people to repent. He wanted them to be judged. That's why he ran in the first place.

"Forty more days and Nineveh will be overturned." Again, there is no indication that he said anything more. What we know is, the citizens responded. News of Jonah's message spread like wildfire. En

masse, the Ninevites declared a fast, donning sackcloth to illustrate the sincerity of their repentance. When word reached the king, he joined in and exchanged robes for rags and sat in the dust while issuing a royal decree that no one, not even animals, was to eat or drink. He declared that all should pray urgently, turn away from evil and foreswear violence. *"Who knows?"* he said. *"God may relent…"*

And God did. *"When God saw what they did and how they turned from their evil ways, he had compassion and did not bring upon them the destruction he had threatened"* (v. 10). This is the most important piece of news in the entire Bible: **when people repent, God relents.** When they ask for forgiveness, He shows compassion. It's great that God is great, but it's essential that He is gracious. Without grace, none of us has a chance. With grace, there is hope for the worst of us.

An Example of Grace

I have some friends, Frank and Julia Mottola, who sit behind me in church each week. Usually they'll enter their row while we're singing the second or third song. Something hard to describe happens inside me every time these two arrive. You could call the feeling "hope." I'm not the most emotionally-in-touch person in the world, but I am moved somehow every time I see Frank and Julia. Their presence reminds me that God really is who He claims to be, a God of mercy, compassion and grace.

You see, a few years ago, Frank committed a moral indiscretion. (I'm not speaking out of turn here; they've shared their story openly in our church.) Julia's heart was broken. It was impossible for her to imagine living with him any longer, but it was almost as impossible to imagine living without him. So they separated. In desperation Frank attended a Christian meeting, where he heard that God was gracious and would forgive him if he asked. Frank invited Christ into his life that night and began seriously pursuing God. He started attending New Song and asked some of our men to pray for a miraculous restoration of his marriage. Through a series of somewhat related circumstances, Julia began attending as well. There was no way she could forgive Frank, but she knew she needed the Lord's

help to get through this devastating trial in her life, so she came week after week after week.

One Sunday, we celebrated communion. If you do the same thing the same way every month, it's easy to let your mind and heart slip into autopilot and just go through the motions, so I try to vary the way we take communion from time to time. This particular Sunday, I decided to add an element. "As you come forward this morning," I said, "I want you to pick up three elements. In addition to the bread and cup, there is also a rock for you with one word on it: *remember*. Sometimes in the Old Testament, God asked His people to take a rock or stack some rocks to remind them of what He had done for them. I want you to take one of these rocks, hold it in your hand and remember what Jesus has done for you."

That was it for Julia. As she held her rock, she thought through all the things Jesus had done for her, and the dam burst. Flooded with tears, she asked His forgiveness, invited Him into her life, and then forgave her husband. She calls that day, "Rock Sunday." (Personally, I think the story itself *rocks*.) The two of them entered into counseling together, re-integrated their family and serve as pillars in our church today. Every Sunday morning they check their daughters into PromiseLand, spend a few minutes encouraging people in the lobby, then take their place in the second row behind me. (I think they actually sit there because they want to support me, like Aaron and Hur holding up Moses' hands.) As I watch them scoot into their seats, I think, "God can forgive anything. God can mend anything," and it gives me hope.

How Do You Respond to a God Like That?

The options for responding to a God who forgives are endless. Jeremiah once said, *"Yet this I call to mind, and therefore I have hope: Because of the Lord's great love we are not consumed, for his compassions never fail. They are new every morning; great is your faithfulness"* (Lamentations 3:21-23). God's grace means it's a new day for you. You can ask Him to forgive you if you need it. You can extend forgiveness to someone else if you've experienced it. You can put your past behind you and look forward to a bright future. You can smile. Like Jonah and the Ninevites, grace means you've got a second chance. How do you want to use that chance today?

NIN´• Ə • FACTS

"Now Nineveh was a very important city – a visit required
three days... Nineveh has more than a hundred and
twenty thousand people who cannot tell their right
hand from their left, and many cattle as well."

Jonah 3:3 & 4:11

Nin´• Ə • facts. (ninƏ fakts) n. pl. Facts related to the ancient city of Nineveh.

If you've ever been to New York City, you know the sensation you get: *big, fast and impressive.* Washington D.C. comes across as *powerful* and *stately.* Tokyo brims with *people.* Combine those three cities and subtract 2,760 years, and you get Nineveh, 760 BC.

The city Jonah entered was the biggest, strongest and wealthiest of its day. Imagine how he must have felt as he reached its outskirts. Nineveh was the capital city of the Assyrian Empire. Named after its chief god *Ashur*, Assyria dominated its region from 900 to 612 BC. Under kings with names like *Tiglath-Pileser* and *Ashurbanipal*, Assyria fine-tuned culture, learning and warfare for almost three centuries. Today, Nineveh's ruins are just outside the Iraqi city of Mosul.

This "Great City" lay 550 miles northeast of Samaria as the crow flies. Of course, crows have never flown that far, and at that time in history, humans lacked the technology to travel across the Arabian Desert.

The heat and lack of water would have killed them. To get to Nineveh, people like Jonah journeyed north up the Mediterranean Coast, then eastward across what is known as "The Fertile Crescent" (the watershed area encompassing the Tigris and Euphrates River Basins). The trip was close to 800 miles. Armies of the era averaged seventeen miles a day. Moving at that rate, Jonah would have reached Nineveh in forty-nine days from Samaria, the capital city of Northern Israel. You can subtract a few days if he departed from one of the ports of Phoenicia, as we speculated a few days ago. At any rate, when Jonah reached this *Great City*, you can bet he was very tanned and very tired.

We learn from 2 Kings 14:25 that Jonah was from a town called Gath Hepher. Gath Hepher was just three miles north of Nazareth, Jesus' home village. One Jewish tradition suggests that Jonah was the son of the widow of Zarephath, whom Elijah raised from the dead[10] (1 Kings 17:8-24). Jonah and Jesus apparently had several things in common!

As far as prophets go, Jonah was a rare breed. Not many of God's spokesmen hailed from Northern Israel. Almost all of Israel's prophets came from the Southern Kingdom of Judah. Our questionable hero is also the refutation of a claim made by the Pharisees. In the book of John, Jesus' contemporaries wanted to prove that Jesus could not be a prophet. During a heated debate, they argued *"Search, and see that no prophet arises out of Galilee"[11]* (John 7:52, NASB). Guess what district Gath Hepher is in? You've got it—Galilee. Not just one but two prophets (Jonah and Jesus) came from there.

The city of Nineveh was protected by two walls. The inner wall was massive: fifty feet wide, one hundred feet tall and eight miles in circumference. The outer wall had a huge circumference[12] of sixty miles, enclosing fields and smaller towns.[13] By ancient standards, the city proper was impervious to attack from large outside forces. But two plagues, one in 765 BC and the other in 759 BC, reminded the

Ninevites of their vulnerability to small inside forces. Some think that these plagues, coupled with a total eclipse of the sun on June 15, 763 BC, were enough to soften the Ninevites to Jonah's preaching. Between 782 BC and 745 BC, Assyria was also engaged in a life and death struggle with the mountain tribes of Urartu to their north.[14] Their possible conquest could have frightened them enough to turn to God. The Bible doesn't specify *why* the Ninevites repented, only that they did so in larger numbers than anywhere else in history. At any rate, the humbling of the Ninevites was a divine work of God's Spirit.

Jonah 4:11 says the city included *"more than a hundred and twenty thousand people who cannot tell their right hand from their left, and many cattle as well."* In comparison, the city of Jerusalem had only thirty thousand inhabitants. The exact population of Nineveh is one of the debates carried on by rusting theologians. Some say "'one hundred twenty thousand' means 'one hundred twenty thousand.'" Others believe the words *"...who cannot tell their right hand from their left"* indicate one hundred twenty thousand people too young to be able to identify their right hand from their left. If that were the case, then to actually support that many young children the total population of greater Nineveh must have been somewhere between six hundred thousand and a million people.

Assyrian Worship

Like their neighbors, the Assyrians worshiped a plurality of gods. How many gods? The estimate is somewhere between three and four thousand.[15] Ashur was their national god, and next in importance was Ishtar, the goddess of fertility and war. Kings built and rebuilt a large shrine to her in downtown Nineveh. Worshipers would come from miles around, but worshiping a goddess of fertility and war presented both dangers and pleasures.

[10] Wilkinson and Boa, *Talk Thru the Bible*, New York: Thomans Nelson, 1983; p. 256.

[11] Hannah, *The Bible Knowledge Commentary*, Old Testament, Wheaton, IL: Victor Books, 1986; p. 1462.

[12] Hannah, *ibid;* p. 1468.

[13] Hannah, *ibid;* p. 1468.

[14] Ellison, *The Expository Bible Commentary, Volume 7*, Grand Rapids: Zondervan, 1985; p. 361.

[15] Anderson, The ZOndervan Pictorial Encyclopedia of the Bible, Volume One, Grand Rapids, MI: ZOndervan, 1978; p.382.

Into this great city stepped one coerced prophet, compelled to be there by the unrelenting greatness of God. The prophet was spared by the grace of God to present the grace of God, which showered on the people like a Rocky Mountain thunderstorm. Every once in a while, something happens at New Song Community Church that is so wonderful, I find myself saying, "Only God could do this!" Jonah 3 is Nineveh's *"Only God..."* day. Who else could get the attention of an entire city? Who else could turn the hearts of every citizen? Who else could speak to one man, who would speak to so many and make such a change? Only God.

How Do You Respond to a God Like That?

One way to respond to a God who sent grace to a city is to ask God to send grace to *your* city. Spend a few minutes asking God to touch the people of your city. Ask Him to touch your mayor and the other civic leaders. Ask God to use you to influence your city. Ask Him to use your pastor and the other pastors of your city to speak words that bring people to repentance and faith.

Habakkuk was a prophet who lived 150 years after Jonah. He read about what God had done in previous generations, then he prayed: *"Lord, I have heard of your fame; I stand in awe of your deeds, O Lord. Renew them in our day, in our time make them known; in wrath, remember mercy"* (Habakkuk 3:2). My paraphrase of Habakkuk's prayer is, *"Lord, do again what you've done in the past; and do it here!"* Maybe you'd like to pray that prayer for your city today.

PUTTING ON SACKCLOTH

"The Ninevites believed God. They declared a fast, and all
of them, from the greatest to the least, put on sackcloth.
When the news reached the king of Nineveh, he rose
from his throne, took off his royal robes, covered himself
in sackcloth and sat down in the dust."

Jonah 3:5–6

I hate corny punch lines, mostly because they stick in your mind far
longer than you'd like. Try to forget them, and they keep returning like
unpaid bills or unwanted facial hair. The one that's stuck in my mind
right now is about a Scot painter who tries to save a little money by
adding water to his paint. One day, while working on the local church
steeple, he finds himself in the middle of a torrential downpour. A clap
of thunder knocks him off his scaffold, slapping him to the ground.
Certain that this is the judgment of God for his miserly shortcuts, the
workman looks up and shouts, "Forgive me Lord, what would you
have me to do?" The reply comes back immediately, in a James Earl
Jones-like voice: "Repaint, and thin no more."

That punch line showed up in my brain while I was reading
Jonah 3:5 this morning. I didn't have to try to retrieve it; it just came.
I couldn't remember the whole joke, so I Googled "repaint and thin
no more," and 47,000 references popped up on the search page. I had
no idea people enjoyed laughing at Scots so much.

Repenting (like repainting) is not a popular activity these days. We
don't like to admit our errors, and repenting involves not just admitting,
but also changing our ways. In ancient times when people repented, they
owned their error and visibly demonstrated remorse by putting on a
special type of clothing called "sackcloth." Sackcloth is a strong, rough

material woven from the long dark hairs of goats or camels.[16] In biblical times, it was used to make grain sacks (Genesis 42:25), saddlebags (Joshua 9:4) and sometimes bedding material (2 Samuel 21:10). Shepherds and other members of the underclass used it for clothing. Since sackcloth was dark in texture and gave no sign of pretense, wearing it showed you were in need or distress. It was the perfect garb for demonstrating sorrow. Its rough, itchy texture reinforced one's feeling of being in a bad way.

Jacob donned sackcloth when he heard that his son Joseph was dead (Genesis 37:34). David commanded Joab and company to wear it at the death of Abner (2 Samuel 3:31). The people of Jerusalem wore it at their great confessional in Nehemiah 9:1. In Matthew 11:21, Jesus told his audience that if His miracles had been performed before the pagans of Tyre and Sidon, they would have *"repented long ago in sackcloth and ashes."*

The people of Nineveh didn't require a miracle to move them to repentance. There was no thunderclap, no voice from heaven, just the solo voice of a reluctant prophet saying, *"You have forty days before your city is going to be overturned."* Those words won hundreds of thousands of hearts, from the peasant on the pavement to the potentate in his palace. Conviction was so palpable you could cut it with a knife. Hearts were so softened you could spread them like butter. The king felt so strongly about the need for mass repentance, he insisted that even the animals suit up in sackcloth. *"Who knows?"* he said, *"God may yet relent and with compassion turn from his fierce anger so that we will not perish"* (Jonah 3:9).

BELIEVING GOD

At first glance, the motivating force behind this mass remorse appears to be fear. True, the Ninevites feared for their lives. Though pagan worshipers, they understood just enough about the One True Living God to believe that He held the power over life and death. However, look again at the story, because fear *isn't* the actual motivating factor. *"On the first day, Jonah started into the city. He proclaimed, 'Forty more days and Nineveh will be overturned.' The Ninevites believed God"* (Jonah 3:4-5). Did you see it? "The Ninevites believed God." They were motivated to repent because they *believed*. Somehow, they saw God for who He

---

[16] Bratt, *The Zondervan Pictorial Encyclopedia of the Bible*, Volume 5, Grand Rapids, MI: Zondervan, 1978 p. 192.

really is, and it sparked a new perspective on who they really were. When you see yourself in comparison to a great and gracious God, you can't help but bow, and sometimes change into more appropriate clothing and place your knees in the dust.

Belief, *right* belief about God and about yourself, is a powerful change-agent. Before he became a prophet, Isaiah had an image in his mind about God. Then one night he encountered the One True Living God. It gave him a clear picture of who God really is, and his response was, *"Woe to me, for I am a man of unclean lips"* (Isaiah 6:5). Isaiah didn't have any sackcloth with him, or you can bet he would have put it on.

Face to face with God, people can't help but believe, and when they do, they want to change. In fact, God is so great that sometimes He doesn't even have to show up in person. He can send a *messenger,* and people will still believe and change. Jonah was the messenger for Nineveh, and people repented in sackcloth and ashes.

What I find most encouraging about Jonah 3 is that the people didn't repent because of God's *greatness*. In Jonah 1, the sailors repented because they saw God's greatness through physical demonstrations of His power. In Jonah 3, people repented because of God's *grace*. Simply because of love, He offered them the opportunity to *"turn from their evil ways"* (Jonah 3:10).

The summer between my sophomore and junior years of high school, the church I attended hired a youth intern named Rick Duncan. Rick took me under his wing. He hung out with me and my friends several times a week, teaching us about the Bible and about living for God. At the end of the summer, he and the other interns put on a little skit. In the skit, they role-played some of the behavior they had witnessed in members of our group. The skit was polite and tasteful, but I saw myself in just about every foul, arrogant and unkind action portrayed on that stage.

That evening, I experienced what the Bible calls "brokenness." Like Isaiah, when I saw my petty self in light of a great and gracious God, I was dying to change. After the skit, Rick counseled with me in the gutter (a fitting place, considering how low I was feeling). We developed a game plan for how I might become a kinder, gentler me, and then we prayed. I asked God's forgiveness and requested His help in making me into a better man.

Psalm 51:17 says, *"The sacrifices of God are a broken spirit; a broken and contrite heart, O God, you will not despise."* Brokenness is a good thing. It hurts like crazy, but it's a good thing to acknowledge the truth about yourself. When we recognize how far we are from perfection, we long to be more like God, and all heaven rejoices. Psalm 34:18 promises, *"The Lord is close to the brokenhearted and saves those who are crushed in spirit."*

How Do You Respond to a God Like That?

One right way to respond to God is to picture Him exactly for who He is. He's perfect. Kind. Generous. Patient. Forgiving. Sinless. Good. Self-controlled. As you picture a God like that, how do you compare to Him?

One day God was talking to Jeremiah about the flaws of the people of his day. God said, *"Are they ashamed of their loathsome conduct? No, they have no shame at all; they do not even know how to blush"* (Jeremiah 8:12). Do you know how to blush? Sometimes blushing, bowing, then asking forgiveness and purposing to change are the best responses to God. Take a minute to think about this question: *Is there anything I need to blush about today?*

Fasting

"The Ninevites believed God. They declared a fast... By decree
of the king and his nobles, do not let any man or beast, herd
or flock, taste anything; do not let them eat or drink."

Jonah 3:5, 7

Fast is a word that's never made much sense to me. According to
everything I know, it should mean "rapid," "quick," or "it'll be over
soon." Anyone who has ever fasted knows that just the opposite is true.
A fast is never rapid, quick or over soon. You can finish dinner at 6:45,
decide you're fasting until the following evening, and by 6:55 you're
craving any morsel your mouth can imagine. Time moves slowly when
you fast. Unless you're a veteran "faster," it's never *over soon*.

One thing's for sure: you have to be serious about fasting. In
a culture saturated with satiating ourselves, fasting takes discipline
and determination. So why are we even bothering to talk about it in
a book on *Jonah*? Because the Ninevites fasted, and it helped them; it
may have even saved their lives. God seems to think fasting is good
for us on occasion. Remember, this is a book on responding to God
in all the right ways, and one of the right ways is by fasting. So put
down that sandwich, and let's talk about fasting for a minute.

Throughout the Bible, there are a variety of reasons why people
fast. Samuel fasted for help in time of war (1 Samuel 7:6). The
Israelites fasted for wisdom about going to war (Judges 20:26).

Jehoshaphat fasted for protection in war (2 Chronicles 20:3). David fasted in hopes that God would spare the life of his son (2 Samuel 12:16); he also fasted as a means of humbling himself (Psalm 35:13). The men of Jabesh fasted to mourn the life of Saul (1 Samuel 31:13). The people of Jerusalem fasted out of sorrow for their sin (Nehemiah 9:1). The people of Nineveh fasted out of desperation for God's forgiveness (Jonah 3:5). Ezra, Nehemiah and Esther fasted as a means of intensifying their prayers (Ezra 8:21; Nehemiah 1:4; Esther 4:16). All Israelites fasted to celebrate certain holy days (Leviticus 23:27). Moses and Daniel fasted in preparation for hearing from God (Exodus 34:28; Daniel 9:3). Early Christian leaders fasted before ordaining elders and commissioning apostles (Acts 13:3; 14:23).

Biblical fasts come in all shapes and sizes. There are secret fasts (Matthew 6:16-18), public fasts (Jeremiah 36:9), community fasts (Nehemiah 9:1), partial fasts (Daniel 10:3), water-only fasts (Matthew 4:2), and no-food-or-water-fasts (Ezra 10:6). In terms of length, there are one night fasts (Daniel 6:18), one day fasts (1 Samuel 7:6), three day fasts (Esther 4:16), week-long fasts (2 Samuel 12:16-23), two-week-long fasts (Acts 27:33-34), three-week-long fasts (Daniel 10:3-13), and forty-day fasts (Exodus 24:18; Matthew 4:2).

Why Should I Fast?

So what will fasting do for you? If your first thought is "help me lose weight," don't bother. While fasting is not a command (and not recommended for people with certain health conditions), Jesus seems to assume the practice will be one of the normal habits of His followers. In Matthew 6:16, he says, *"When you fast…"* meaning, "Not if, but *when…*" Later, in Luke 5:34-35, He says, *"Can you make the guests of the bridegroom fast while he is with them? But the time will come when the bridegroom will be taken from them; in those days they will fast."* Personally, there are four reasons and seasons when I fast.

1. I fast when I want to reinforce my love for and dependency on God. Midway through a day-long fast, my stomach starts whispering, "Why are we fasting again?" My mind replies, "To remind ourselves that we don't live by bread alone, but are absolutely dependent on God for everything." My whole

body then reasons, "You must really love God to be doing this." My mind answers, "I do."

This kind of fast also loosens materialism's grip on me. Thirty minutes after beginning a fast, I start thinking about food. It owns me. Including snacks, I usually bow to it three to five times a day. While I'm fasting, food doesn't own me; God does. After completing a fast, food has less ownership of me, and so do "things." Fasting is a means for learning to live without "stuff." At the end of a fast, God owns me more and "stuff" owns me less.

2. I fast when I want to hear from God.
Three or four times a year, I retreat to a friend's cabin to hear from God about my life, my family and the church I lead. I find that I am able to hear God's voice better when there is no food in my stomach. The key to this kind of fast is the combination of fasting, prayer and solitude. I have tried to fast and hear from God while carrying on a normal day's work; it doesn't work for me. On the other hand, getting away with an empty stomach with a Bible, notepad and no distractions works very well for me.

3. I fast when I want to increase my self-discipline.
The Apostle Paul clued me into this secret when he said, *"I beat my body and make it my slave so that after I have preached to others, I myself will not be disqualified for the prize"* (1 Corinthians 9:27). I have discovered that discipline transfers from one aspect of my life to another. The ability to say "no" to food translates into a heightened ability to say "no" to temptation as well.

4. I fast when I want to intensify my prayers.
A year before moving to Oceanside to start New Song Community Church, I knew I would need a first-class music leader who could relate to artists. A church like ours can't function without the arts. This position was so important to me that for six months, I fasted every Monday morning until God supplied Free Grafton, the perfect man for the job.

God expects us to fast from time to time but not as a means of torture or punishment. He understands how we work better than we do. He is great and gracious, so if He thinks fasting is good for us, fasting *must* be good for us. I'd be the last one to suggest that you ought to go overboard with fasting. Still, I'd like to be one of the voices that helps add fasting to your spiritual diet.

How Do You Respond to a God Like That?

How might fasting fit into your lifestyle? How can you maximize it as a tool to get closer to God? Would you like to try fasting, prayer and solitude as a means to hear His voice? Do you think a half-day's fast might increase your self-discipline? Might fasting become a tool to intensify your prayers? I hope you'll pick a reason to fast and a day (or a half-day) to try it, and see what happens. Who knows? You might find that the time goes by really *fast*.

THE SIGN OF JONAH

"Then some of the Pharisees and teachers of the law said to
him, 'Teacher, we want to see a miraculous sign from you.'
He answered, 'A wicked and adulterous generation asks for a
miraculous sign! But none will be given it except the sign of
the prophet Jonah. For as Jonah was three days and nights in
the belly of a huge fish, so the Son of Man will be three
days and three nights in the heart of the earth. The men
of Nineveh will stand up at the judgment with this
generation and condemn it; for they repented at the
preaching of Jonah, and now one greater than Jonah is here.'"

Matthew 12:38-41

There's a sign over our bathtub that reads "St. George." I know, most
people don't hang signs over their bathtubs. The Seeds are a little
kitschy that way, but the sign has a story behind it. A few years ago,
Lori and I took a trip to the Canadian Maritime Provinces. (That's
Nova Scotia, New Brunswick and Prince Edward Island, for you non-
Canadians.) What began as a leisurely vacation escalated into an all-out
quest. My wife loves all things French and has always wanted to hang
an antique French street sign somewhere in our house. The Maritimes
were once populated with French-speakers. They were flushed out
and transported to Louisiana a couple hundred years ago, but that's
another story. Many Maritimers still speak French, and several French
street names still linger, so we were going to bag a French sign and
bring it home.

We came away empty from Nova Scotia. We poked our heads
into antique stores in Kentville, Annapolis Royal, Digby and parts in
between. Nada, nothing, no sign of street signs. We struck out. However,
Nova Scotia was settled by the Scots, whereas New Brunswick was

originally French. Hope sprang eternal as we ferried from Digby to Saint John. The search intensified as we drove north to Fredericton, then east to Moncton. Didn't these people ever discard street signs? We crossed the bridge onto Prince Edward Island, which is the land of the English and Anne of Avonlea, so our hopes diminished. We only had one day left before heading home. Prince Edward Island is pure, pristine beauty in July. Lori would vacation there every summer if she could.

At a little crossroads, our hearts elevated when we saw a dilapidated old building reading "ANTIQUES" beside a cute little cottage. It was locked up with a notice that read, "Closed to Visitors." *"Hope deferred makes the heart sick"* (Proverbs 13:12a). We poked our noses against the window. Not twenty feet inside was a quaint little antique sign reading "St. George." It wasn't in French, but it would do nicely—if only we could get to it!

Lori tapped on the cottage door to find out why someone would have an antique shop that was closed to visitors. No one responded. She crossed the road and asked her question to a smiling clerk at the country store. "Oh, that's Davey Jones' place. Davey doesn't do live business anymore—he's discovered eBay," she said. "You can give him a call if you like, but I don't think he's home today."

Lori took the phone number and tried it. The clerk was right; nobody was home. We drove on to the next town, knowing we'd be flying home sign-less. This little town housed a Tim Horton's (Canada's answer to Starbucks). We stopped in for lunch and a little commiseration. "We were so close!" Lori lamented. Always the optimist, I said, "It's been forty minutes, and there's a pay-phone outside, why don't you try Davey's number again?" With nothing to lose, Lori rolled three coins into the pay-phone slot and dialed Davey. Three rings...and then an answer! "Hello, this is Davey."

"Hi Davey, my name is Lori Seed. I know your store is closed, but my husband and I peeked in your window and saw a sign that we'd like to buy. Is there any way we could persuade you to sell it to us? We're down here at Tim Horton's and will be leaving the island this afternoon."

"Tim Horton's, you say?"

"Yes, the one about fifteen minutes from your house."

"Get me a medium creme and a walnut crunch and I'll open up and sell you the sign."

So that's what we did. We paid for "St. George" with a gift from Tim Horton's, the remainder of our Canadian pocket change and a few American dollars. Davey told us the story behind our sign. "I got it at an old railroad station they were tearing down in New Brunswick. If you look closely, you can see the outline of an older sign underneath. The sign used to read, 'Utopia Camp.' The Canadian Army opened a training camp near St. George during World War II. The camp closed in 1954. The railroad salvaged the sign, painted over it and used it as its own."

So we dragged the sign home on the plane and nailed it to our bathroom wall. It's there as proof we've been to the Maritimes. *"Hope deferred makes the heart sick, but a longing fulfilled is a tree of life"* (Proverbs 13:12).

During Jesus' earthly ministry, the Pharisees wanted proof that He was the Messiah. "Give us a sign," they said. "The only sign I have for you is the sign of Jonah," Jesus replied. *"As Jonah was three days and nights in the belly of a huge fish, so the Son of Man will be three days and three nights in the heart of the earth."* A few weeks later, Jesus went to the Cross. They wrapped His body in burial clothes and entombed it in a fresh-hewn grave. Three days later[17] He emerged from the tomb on Easter morning. If you're looking for a sign, you've found it. It's what Christ called "the sign of Jonah."

---

[17] "Three days and three nights" is Hebrew idiom that requires only a portion of the first and thrd days. "In Jewish thought, a day and night make an "onah," a part of an onah is as the whole." D.A. Carson, *The Expository Bible Commentary*, Volume 8, Grand Rapids, MI: ZOndervan, 1984; p. 296.

Jonah and Jesus have a lot in common. Both spent three days entombed. Both were delivered from death. Both preached to crowds of people. Jonah saw large numbers repent; Jesus, not as many, which is why Jesus says, *"The men of Nineveh will stand up at the judgment with this generation and condemn it."* They were given a sign. They didn't have to peek in a window for it, make phone calls for it, buy Tim Horton's for it or pay for it. It was all done for them.

Why Jesus Came

In 760 BC, a great and gracious God sent a prophet to the people of Nineveh. Before completing his mission, the prophet spent three days and nights in the belly of a big fish. When people heard his message they believed, in part, because the fish-miracle proved his divine commission. That's the sign *underneath* the sign of Jesus. God came to the Ninevites because He couldn't stand the thought of them spending eternity without Him. He also came because He wanted to create a sign that could later be painted over by Jesus and used as His own.

The story of Jonah is that God so loved Nineveh that He sent a reluctant prophet, so that whoever would believe might not perish, but have life. The story of Jesus is the same, except, in Jesus' words, *"… now one greater than Jonah is here."* For God so loved the *world* that He sent His one and only Son, that whoever would believe might not perish, but have everlasting life. *"Now one greater than Jonah is here."* He is here for *you*.

How Do You Respond to a God Like That?

The best response is to bow and thank Him. Or, if you have not yet expressed belief in Him, today is your day. Say to Him, "Lord, I believe. I want everlasting life. Forgive my sins, I am turning from them today and inviting You to lead me from now on."

If you've prayed that prayer, I have good news for you. Your sin is now painted over. Where it once read "GUILTY," now it reads "FORGIVEN."

Week 4 | Jonah 4

*R*ESPONDING TO GOD'S CORRECTION (AGAIN)

Responding to God's Correction—Again

"Then the Lord provided a vine and made it grow up over
Jonah to give shade for his head to ease his discomfort, and
Jonah was very happy about the vine. But at dawn the next
day God provided a worm, which chewed the vine so that it
withered. When the sun rose, God provided a scorching
east wind, and the sun blazed on Jonah's head so
that he grew faint. He wanted to die…"

Jonah 4:6-8

My children were born thirteen months apart. Bryan could walk
before Amy could crawl. Those first few months after we brought our
daughter home from the hospital, our son was in what psychologists
label, "the oral stage." This little guy loved his new sister. He loved
her so much he would often waddle over and bite her. Poor Amy! She
couldn't escape. She just lay there, like dessert on a platter.

We tried reasoning with Bryan. "Son, it hurts when you bite
Amy. Please don't do it again." We tried sending him to his room.
"Bryan, you can't do that anymore. It makes Amy cry. Go to your
room and we'll come to get you in a few minutes. For now, you're
in time out." We tried spanking him. "Son, I'm sorry to have to do
this, but you *must* learn not to bite your sister." Nothing worked. As
a young father, I was at the end of my wisdom.

Fortunately, there were more experienced fathers in my church.
One said, "This is going to sound harsh, but at his stage, Bryan can't
imagine how much it hurts Amy when he bites her. The only way for
him to learn is for *you* to bite *him*. Try this: as soon as he bites her,
you bite him in exactly the same place. If he bites her on the cheek,
bite him on the cheek. If he bites her on the hand, bite him on the

hand. I guarantee he'll stop biting her—*fast*." It sounded crazy. Bite my son? Not having any better plan, I bit him. You can call the Child Protection people on me, but it worked. Within five days of our "bite for bite" strategy, Bryan's oral fixation was, well, *fixed*.

Learning the Lesson

If you study the mass of humanity, you can see that some people learn their lessons the first time. For instance, Moses took a man's life. After God's work with him in the wilderness, He never took a second. David committed adultery. The pain it caused cured him once and for all. However, other people never learn: Saul never got over his moodiness. Nabal remained a fool all his days. Still others learn their lessons and revert. Jonah was one of those. His experience in the school-of-the-fish fixed him—temporarily. He purposed to obey (Jonah 2:9), then backslid into belligerence again (Jonah 4).

In chapter four, Jonah is one peeved prophet. He's headstrong and impudent, acting more like a two-year-old than a man of God. Fortunately, this second rebellion didn't involve direct disobedience, just overt insolence. His disdain for the Ninevites reeked and leaked. Perched on a hillside, he fumed, "I'm mad enough to die!"

I love how God never deserts us in need, and He never indulges our immaturities. He *abounds* in love. With father-like affection, God repeats lessons and brings out new methods to ensure the growth of His children. In chapter one, the Lord employs a wind, a storm and a fish for Jonah's correction. In chapter four, He summons a vine, a worm and a sirocco for the same purpose.

Enraged beyond all reason, Jonah mounts a hill east of the city to await the Assyrians' fate. God had promised a forty-day grace period before unleashing His wrath, and Jonah hopes against hope that the Ninevites will do something to speed up the clock. It's hot on his hillside, so he builds himself a lean-to, which probably was just a few upright poles with palm fronds laid over them. This flimsy shelter doesn't block much wind or sun, so Jonah develops sunburn to go with his heartburn.

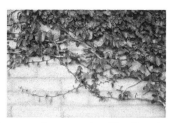

This is where God comes in— again. The Lord sends him a second miracle: a fast-growing vine that shields his shelter from the elements. Jonah leans back and gets comfortable. "This is more like it," he says. He smiles for the first time in a long time. Chapter four's vine-miracle is a lot like the fish-miracle of chapter two. Jonah 4:6 says that God *"provided"* the vine just like he had *"provided"* the fish. Botanists believe this vine was a castor-bean plant; most likely a variety called *Ricinus communis*. Ricinus has big leaves and thrives in the heat, and its stalk is very susceptible to damage. A few bites from the right worm, and it's toast.

Castor-bean plants can grow to twelve feet, and they can grow very quickly. Jonah 4:7 says, *"The Lord God... made it grow up over Jonah to give shade to his head..."* Apparently, the growth took place in one night. God sometimes combines supernatural forces with natural ones to accomplish His miracles. Jesus did this in John 2 when He took water and made it into wine. Given enough time, that same water could have become wine by pouring it on a grapevine. Jesus accelerated the process to meet the time-demand. In the same way, God could have let nature take its course and have the vine grow at normal speed. But Jonah needed a lesson, so God juiced the process. Like an athlete on steroids, this plant got big *in a hurry*. With the plant in place, things seemed to be going Jonah's way.

He was resting and happy until God "provided" a worm to wither the plant. For the second time, Jonah described himself as "mad enough to die."

God Speaks

The Lord's conversation with Jonah at the end of the chapter reminds me of some of my conversations with my children. When they reached a certain age, we stopped sending them to their rooms and started sitting down for heart-to-heart talks. Jonah 4:9-11 reads to me like one of those talks. God tries to help Jonah see the smallness of his thinking. *"Jonah, did the plant really mean that much to you? It only lived for a day. You didn't put any effort into it. If you feel this badly about it, how much worse would you feel if you had planted, watered, and cared for it? My son, see those people down there? I made them. I have nurtured and cared for them since long before you were born. I love the Ninevites. Your pain over the loss of the plant is nothing compared to mine when I think about their destruction.[18]"* You can almost hear the tenderness in God's voice. He's treating Jonah graciously, like He treated the Ninevites.

This is how God treats every wanderer who is willing to sit and listen to Him. His greatness won't let you get away with hurting yourself or harming others, nor will it let Him watch you waste your life on hissy-fits or poor attitudes. When he corrects, it's always for your benefit. If you learn the lesson, you get to move on. If you forget the lesson, He'll bring you back to it again (and again and again and again, if necessary). He is a great and gracious God.

How Do You Respond to a God Like That?

No healthy parent ever enjoys disciplining his or her child. We initiate it because we want the child to grow. In an ideal world, your children would understand this and thank you for caring enough to correct them. I want to suggest that you can make this world more ideal by responding to God the way you would want your children to respond to you.

Is there something you're going through right now that has you feeling like the Father is doing some correcting or redirecting in your life? James 1:3 says, *"Consider it pure joy, my brothers, whenever you face trials of many kinds, because you know that the testing of your faith develops perseverance. Perseverance must finish its work so that you may be mature and complete, not lacking anything."* If what you're experiencing feels like some form of correction, you can be sure there is also some form of growth taking place within you. The right response to God in such circumstances is to;

---

[18] Adapted from Donald Bakers, as quoted in Walvoord and Zuck, *The Bible Knowledge Commentary, Old Testament*, Wheaton, IL: Victor Books, 1986, P. 1472.

1. Remember that your Father loves you

2. Try your best to learn whatever lesson is being taught

3. Thank Him for loving you enough to walk with you through the pain.

I hope you don't need this lesson on correction today. Inevitably though, someday you will. So underline that last sentence (the one beginning with "The right response…") and apply it when you need it.

GETTING MAD AT GOD

"But Jonah was greatly displeased and became angry...'
I am angry enough to die.'"

Jonah 4:1, 9

I was twenty-three years old. For weeks I had been praying very specifically about God's provision and direction in my life, and it seemed like He was ignoring me. I couldn't feel His presence or see any way in which He was at work in my life. For days I talked with him about this, and then one night, I got beet-red mad.

Long after dark, I found the privacy of a golf course fairway (so I wouldn't be interrupted) and poured my heart out. I listed all the things I wanted and didn't have, and I told God how frustrated and disappointed I felt. Then I looked heavenward and said, "Lord, I know You too well to say anything stupid. I don't want to blaspheme or walk away from You. But right now I am so mad at You that, instead of saying something I'll regret later, I'm not going to say anything at all. For the next week You won't hear from me. I'm going to be ignoring You because it's the only means I can think of to express how angry I am."

It was a brilliant plan, so brilliant that I spent the next seven days telling God *what I wasn't going to tell Him.* Four or five times a day I found myself saying, "Lord, You know that I'm not talking to You this week, but if I was..." and then I would spill out all my thoughts. My conversations with God that week were some of the most fervent and poignant I have ever had. Yes, besides being ridiculous, the idea of ignoring God was foolish and petty. But I learned a lot that week:

What I Learned By Not Talking to God

- **God knows what you're thinking, whether you say it to Him or not.** Since you can't hide your thoughts from Him, you might as well discuss them with Him.

- **You can't force God's hand.** You will never be able to trick, deceive, bargain or manipulate God into granting requests that aren't good for you. If He's not granting your request, you can believe the request isn't what you *really* want. God only gives good gifts to His children.

- **The Lord loves to hear from you when you're hurting.** He's an ever-present help in time of trouble. Your prayers don't always have to be about getting something from God. He appreciates hearing your thoughts and feelings and loves processing them with you.

- **Being mad can be a motivator.** Sometimes the intense feelings generated by anger can move you to do the thing you thought was too hard or too much work. If what you're wanting is obviously wrong, then give it up; but if you're praying for something that you know God wants for you, apply yourself diligently, and you may achieve it. Sometimes God doesn't answer your prayers because He knows you have more capacity. When parents do everything for their child, the child never learns the joy of hard work and self-accomplishment. If your request is righteous, instead of just getting mad, get determined and do something about it. Your effort may be the answer you're praying for.

- **Sometimes God gives you lessons so you can share them with others.**

Jonah's Anger

At the beginning of Jonah 4, Jonah is hotter than a hornet. He's so mad he can't function. (Maybe that's why they call it "madness"?)

He directs his frustration heavenward. *"Lord,"* he says, *"is this not what I said when I was still at home? That is why I was so quick to flee to Tarshish. I knew that you are a gracious and compassionate God, slow to anger and abounding in love, a God who relents from sending calamity"* (Jonah 4:2).

In Exodus 33, Moses asked God to show him His glory. In response, God revealed himself to Moses and recited His full name. *"And [God] passed in front of Moses, proclaiming, 'The Lord, the Lord, the compassionate and gracious God, slow to anger and abounding in love and faithfulness, maintaining love to thousands and forgiving wickedness, rebellion and sin'"* (Exodus 34:6-7). Jonah quoted this prayer in Jonah 4:2, but did you catch what Jonah left out? You don't see the "forgiving wickedness, rebellion and sin" part. Essentially, Jonah is saying, "I am mad because you forgave these wicked, rebellious, sinful people. I wanted you to condemn them. I was hoping you would wipe them from the face of the earth. They have treated my people so badly; I wanted you to *terminate* them. The last thing they deserved was Your forgiveness, which is why I ran the other direction in the first place. Now, they're not only still alive; I may have to put up with them in heaven some day!"

Jonah was unspeakably mad, and who could blame him? If you've ever *really* hated somebody, you know how Jonah felt. The Assyrians were Public Enemy Number One. They were the bullies on the Middle Eastern block, the gang-members who made it dangerous to go out at night. They were a big threat to Israel's freedom and prosperity. In fact in 722 BC, thirty-eight years after Jonah preached to Nineveh, the army of Assyria pillaged the kingdom of Northern Israel, laid siege to Samaria and dragged every last citizen into captivity. Assyria's assimilation strategy was to inter-mix their conquered peoples in order to erase each one's former national identity. 2 Kings 19:24 reads, *"The king of Assyria brought people from Babylon, Cuthah, Avva, Hamath and Sepharvaim and settled them in the towns of Samaria to replace the Israelites."* After 722 BC, there was no "Northern Israel," or northern tribes of Israel—only the southern Israelites remained. So in a way, Jonah contributed to Israel's destruction. His preaching preserved the Assyrian's capital city. If Nineveh had been destroyed, Israel may have been preserved.

Using Anger Constructively

What is the right way to respond to your anger? The next time you're angry, try focusing your energy on something positive. For instance, what if Jonah had channeled his anger toward serving his friends instead of cursing his enemies? What if, instead of pouting, he had used his pent up power to preach to his fellow Israelites? After all, the reason they were wiped out was because of their unfaithfulness to God. How different would history look if Jonah had caused the type of revival at home that he had caused in Nineveh?

I wish I could say that God used my week of "madness" to do something constructive, but I can't. He did graciously use that week to teach me some lessons I'll never forget. Two things I love about God:

1. He's *great* enough to absorb my anger without feeling threatened by it.

2. He's *gracious* enough to love and listen to me in the midst of it.

How Do You Respond to a God Like That?

The next time you're struck by madness, talk to God about it. He's big enough to handle your emotions, and He already knows how you feel. You'll find He's an excellent listener. And, if you're able, try channeling your elevated energy level into something constructive. Ultimately, as you'll see later, I think that's what Jonah did.

THE MESSAGE OF JONAH

"Should I not be concerned about that great city?"

Jonah 4:11b

This four-chapter Minor Prophet is unique within his ranks. Most prophetic books record the spoken words of the prophet who wrote them. The book of Jonah is forty-eight verses long, and only one of those verses contains a message spoken by its prophet. The book of Jonah says more about the messenger than his message.

Jonah's forty-eight verses trace the path of a reluctant prophet overruled by a great God. God's agenda is to communicate His love to people (the Ninevites) who are outside the family of faith. Jonah's agenda is to stay home with the people he loves. God's focus is on those who are outside the community; Jonah's focus is on those who are inside it. God is a ***Next-Door*** God; Jonah is an at-home prophet. In the end, of course, God wins. He uses whatever means necessary to get His message to those outside the family, and they respond.

Sadly, the Jonah-story is not too different from what has been going on between God and His Church for the last few decades. God, who so loved the *world*, wants to use His Church to reach the *world*. The Church, made up of people who know and love each other, sometimes just wants to use the Church to help its *members*. In other words, God has an *outward focus*, while church members tend to have an *inward focus*. The message of Jonah is *God loves the whole world.* That includes people living in Africa; it also includes people living next door. Oh, how God longs for us to love our neighbors as ourselves!

A quick study through the Bible confirms how much God loves cities. One time, Jesus stood on a hillside overlooking Jerusalem and broke down weeping over it (Luke 19:41). Jeremiah tells the captives who are being deported to Babylon, *"Seek the peace and prosperity of the city to which I have carried you in exile. Pray to the Lord for it..."* (Jeremiah 29:7). Proverbs 11:11 claims that *"Through the blessing of the upright a city is exalted..."* It's automatic: if a city is to be safe and healthy, it must have righteous people involved in it. Imagine what it would be like if masses of people turned to Christ in your city? Imagine what it would be like if masses of Christians got involved in community affairs, influencing the crime rate, literacy rate and homelessness factors. Such a dream might be worthy of a few minutes of prayer each morning.

The message of Jonah is that God loves all peoples so much that He will go to extraordinary lengths to reach them. His means of reaching people is always people. John 3:16 says, *"For God so loved the world that he gave his one and only Son, that whoever believes in him shall not perish but have eternal life."* The message of Jonah is this same John 3:16 message, 760 years before its time. Paul tells the Corinthians, *"God, who reconciled us to himself, gave us the ministry of reconciliation"* (2 Corinthians 5:18). Imagine what it will be like when all the Jonahs finish their business with fishes and plants and say, "Here am I, Lord. Use me." I believe that day is coming.

MORE SUB-MESSAGES IN JONAH

Another sub-message is that *if God loves all peoples, then no one is beyond hope.* You know the busybody down the block? One conversation or small act of kindness might be all she needs to come to Christ. You know the know-it-all at the office? He may not be as far from God's love as you think. How about the aunt or uncle in your family? The one you hope to avoid sitting next to at the Thanksgiving table? If thousands of Ninevites can repent after an eight-word sermon, surely these people can be touched by God's love.

A third sub-message is that *God specializes in second chances.* Jonah gets a second chance to be used by God. You do too. If you've been on the sidelines for awhile, maybe it's time to get back in God's game.

How Do You Respond to a God Like That?

I recommend you start with prayer. Before you talk to your neighbors about Jesus, talk to Jesus about your neighbors. Before your church goes next door, ask God to prepare the way before you. Here's a prayer you could utter every morning in less time than it takes to walk from your bedroom to your car:

Lord, would You give me Your heart for my neighbors? Would You give me Your heart for my city? Use me and my church to reach them, however You will.

THE FIRST AND LAST WORD

The word of the Lord came to Jonah son of Amittai,
"Go to the great city of Nineveh and preach against it..."

Jonah 1:1

But the Lord said... "Should I not be concerned
about that great city?"

Jonah 4:10-11

If you had asked me a few months ago, "Who is the main character in the book of Jonah?" I would have said, "Jonah, of course." He's the one who runs, gets swallowed, preaches and pouts. Besides, his name is on the book. Now that we've walked through the text, you and I both know better. *God* is the main character of the story. In the story of Jonah, He:

1. Commanded Jonah to preach (Jonah 1:1)
2. Sent a great wind (Jonah 1:4)
3. Listened to the sailors' prayer (Jonah 1:14)
4. Turned the hearts of the sailors (Jonah 1:16)
5. Provided the great fish (Jonah 1:17)
6. Listened to Jonah's prayer (Jonah 2:2)
7. Commanded the fish to vomit Jonah (Jonah 2:10)
8. Commanded Jonah to preach again (Jonah 3:1)
9. Turned the hearts of the Ninevites (Jonah 3:5)
10. Turned the heart of the king (Jonah 3:6)
11. Relented from sending destruction (Jonah 3:10)

12. Listened to Jonah's prayer again (Jonah 4:1)

13. Counseled with Jonah (Jonah 4:4)

14. Provided a vine (Jonah 4:6)

15. Provided a worm (Jonah 4:7)

16. Provided a scorching east wind (Jonah 4:8)

17. Counseled with Jonah again (Jonah 4:9)

18. Reasoned with Jonah about the Ninevehites (Jonah 4:10-11)

That's eighteen actions in forty-eight verses. He gets top billing, hands-down. In addition, look closely and you'll see that God speaks the first and last words in the book.

In a country like America, where we are entitled to equal rights and equal footing, the idea that someone—God—might be "in charge," creates a little tension. We want God to be our friend. We want Him to be accessible. We like to come to Him when we're hurting, pray to Him when we're needy, and watch Him work when we're helpless. Jonah points out that God is *"...a gracious and compassionate God, slow to anger and abounding in love"* (Jonah 4:2). That's His grace shining through.

But God is something else as well. Throughout this study, we've labeled the other side of God as *greatness*. Let me use a synonym for that before we close: God is *sovereign*. He is the absolute ruler of heaven and earth. He has both power and authority over the affairs of men. Paul says, *"The God who made the world and everything in it is the Lord of heaven and earth... He himself gives all men life and breath and everything else. From one man he made every nation of men... and he determined the exact times set for them and the exact places where they should live"* (Acts 17:24-26).

I live just south of Marine Corps Camp Pendleton. Anyone familiar with the military knows the Commanding General's Protocol. When the General speaks, you respond. When the General stands and says, "Thank you," the meeting is over. The man in charge always has the first and last word. Turn to the first book of the Bible, and you'll see that God has the first word: *"In the beginning, God created the heavens and the earth...And God said, 'Let there be light,' and there was light"* (Genesis 1:1, 3). Turn to the last book in the Bible, and you'll see that God has the last word, *"Yes, I am coming soon"* (Revelation 22:20). He not only *has* the first and last word, the Bible indicates He is the first and last word: *"I am the Alpha and the Omega, the First and the Last, the Beginning and the End"* (Revelation 22:13).

HOW DO YOU RESPOND TO A GOD LIKE THAT?

Here are some suggestions:

- With loyalty
- With obedience
- With reverence
- With silence
- With honor
- With humility
- With gratitude
- With awe
- With respect
- With_____

The truth is, we can't respond to a God like this as fully as He deserves, because He deserves so much more than we have to give. But we *can* respond with *all* that we have to give. How would you like to respond to Him today? Before you close this book, take a few minutes to do what's in your heart right now.

THE END?

"But the Lord said, 'You have been concerned about this
vine, though you did not tend it or make it grow. It sprang up
overnight and died overnight. But Nineveh has more than a
hundred twenty thousand people who cannot tell their right
hand from their left, and many cattle as well. Should I not be
concerned about that great city?"

Jonah 4:10-11

The Book of Jonah may be unique in classic literature. Most stories
follow a predictable progression. For instance, when certain chemistry
develops between the leading man and woman, you *know* they'll get
married in the end; you can see it coming. You start writing the
conclusion in your mind long before the author takes you there.
When a sports team gets on a roll, you can't help but project out to
the end of the season. You can see the championship in your mind
pages before the author writes it in. But in Jonah, apart from almost
all other classic pieces of literature, you *don't* see the end coming.
You *can't* see the end, because the book doesn't end like you know it
should.

Jonah's book is scripted like a four-act play. Act One is staged
onboard a ship as Jonah moves from disobedience to discipline. The
prophet hears God's command and heads the opposite direction. Act
Two unfolds inside the fish, where Jonah responds to the discipline
with a decision to obey. Act Three builds to an incredible climax
as Jonah's personal decision to obey multiplies into thousands of
decisions to obey when the entire city turns to God. As you read
this plotline, you can't help but script the ending. It's obvious; any
ten-year-old could write Act Four. The only possible conclusion to

such a supernatural revival is an incredible celebration. You wrote it in your mind the minute you heard the Ninevites' response to God. It went something like this:

> *And Jonah and all the people knelt and prayed and then stood and worshiped. They encouraged one another and gave gifts to one another. The king decreed that henceforth this day should be celebrated as the great day of the Lord for all time. In all the land, none rejoiced more than Jonah the prophet. End of story, roll the credits.*

But that isn't what happens. Jonah doesn't rejoice; he mourns. He clinches his fists and pounds them on the ground, like a three-year-old throwing his best tantrum. Look at Jonah 4:1, *"But Jonah was greatly displeased and became angry."* The prophet is piqued because the people are pardoned. Who could have predicted this? Where else in history has the good guy won and responded so poorly?

Back in chapter three, God is angry about the Ninevites' violence and mistreatment of others. When they repent, He cools off. When He cools off, Jonah heats up. (The Hebrew for "Jonah… became angry" literally reads, "Jonah… became hot.") The first plot twist we couldn't foresee is Jonah's tantrum. He shouldn't be displeased; he should be delighted. The second plot twist is God's reaction. You'd expect Him to be mad that Jonah is mad. But the Lord, who is slow to anger and abounding in love, abounds in love for Jonah. Like a patient father, He prepares to re-teach the obedience lesson of chapter two.

No Ending

The third plot twist isn't an actual plot twist, and this is where the book becomes unique. After all this, you expect some sort of ending, some sort of resolution. But there is no ending; there is no resolution. The book doesn't end; it just stops. God says, *"Nineveh has more than a hundred and twenty thousand people who cannot tell their right hand from their left, and many cattle as well"* (Jonah 4:11). That's the end of a sentence, not the ending of a story. The book doesn't tell what happened to Jonah, or the Ninevites, or God. How many other stories do you know that have no ending? I'll wager not many; maybe none besides this one. Why doesn't God give us an ending to the story?

As you read through the story, you might notice a similarity between the first and second halves of Jonah. Part of what we learn from the Book of Jonah is that God's children often get a second chance. In chapter three, Jonah gets a second chance to obey. In chapter four, Jonah gets a second chance to learn to love.

The repeated second chances aren't the only parallels:

In Jonah 1, Jonah has the opportunity to change Nineveh! In Jonah 4, Jonah has the opportunity to celebrate the change of Nineveh!

In Jonah 1, God sends a "great wind." In Jonah 4, God sends a "scorching wind."

- In Jonah 1, Jonah is rescued from nature by a fish-miracle. In Jonah 4, Jonah is rescued from nature by a plant-miracle.

- In Jonah 2, Jonah prays for deliverance. In Jonah 4, Jonah prays against deliverance.

- In Jonah 2, Jonah huddles inside a fish-belly. In Jonah 4, Jonah huddles inside a lean-to.

- In Jonah 2, Jonah learns his lesson. In Jonah 4, does Jonah learn his lesson again? We'll never know.

The book of Jonah ends with the prophet sitting outside the city, wrestling with the Lord. There is no record of what Jonah did. Why? I believe it's because God recorded this story for *you and me*. The book finishes open-ended with an opportunity. Every child of God can place him or herself in the story and decide how they want *their* story to end. It's as if God is asking, "How will *you* respond to me?"

Over the past twenty days, we've experimented with dozens of ways to respond to God. We've created a broad list of responses but not a complete list. I suspect there are as many right ways to respond to God as there are people on the planet and days in which to live. The Book of Jonah ends with a pointed challenge: God has been teaching His child to obey.

From here, you must complete the story. Of all the responses to God, obedience is the most fundamental and maybe the most challenging. The Book of Jonah ends with an obvious question: *Does this child of God obey in what the Lord has asked him/her to do?* The way to begin is by asking, "What has God asked me to do?"

How Do You Respond to a God Like This?

If you're perplexed about Jonah's outcome, I have a ray of hope for you. There must be a reason for the great number of similarities between the first and second halves of Jonah. I think they're there to hint at Jonah's response to God. At the end of Jonah 2, Jonah is commissioned by God to bring a life-changing message to a large group of people. At the end of Jonah 4, is it possible that Jonah is commissioned to bring another life-changing message to another large group of people? If so, who is this large group of people? And where is the message?

I believe *the Book of Jonah* is the second message Jonah preached. Why else would Jonah publish such a humiliating autobiography? If I'm right, then Jonah's second message has been more effective than his first. After all, how many lives do you suppose this little book has changed over the past 2,760 years? And if I am right, then this is the underlying message to you and me: no matter where you are with God right now and no matter what you've done, He can still use you. After Jonah's repeated disobedience, God used him to touch more lives the second time than the first.

If you will let Him, the Lord will use you more powerfully than you've ever been used before. So...

How Will You Respond to a God Like This?

AFTERWORD

By Amy Seed

Afterword

By Amy Seed

As the warm evening air of Mexicali, Mexico swept across the dusty plain of our campsite, the team assembled in our dust-ridden lawn chairs around a small wooden cross under a blanket of stars and a moon so clear it seemed like the man on it was waiting to talk to you. That was the night I died to myself. Although the cross was small, it is the place where I was crucified. Not in any ghastly sense, but in a spiritual one.

We were each given a small scrap of white paper and the question, "What is one thing you are going to leave in Mexico?" After a week of partaking in outrageously supernatural ministry to the Mexican people, I had experienced God's power and peace in a very real way. Yet, in the midst of deliberation and internal conflict, I stood, tears streaming down my sun-darkened, 16-year-old cheeks before the forty high-school students and confessed, "For the past seven years I have been fighting God over my future." Thus, I surrendered by explaining my own plans of becoming an Interior Designer instead of a missionary, and I speared my scrap of paper through the small nail protruding from the dusty wooden cross. Like Jonah, I had ignored God in an attempt to pursue my personal interests, and God had finally grabbed hold of me.

Maybe you're in the same place. Perhaps you have read this book and discovered some areas that need growth in your life. Maybe you are stuck in a spiritual rut and frustrated because you don't know why you aren't progressing like almost every other "good Christian" you know. Maybe you aren't running away from God's plan for you and boarding the ship for Tarshish, but you definitely aren't moving toward Nineveh. You're caught in the treacherous middle-ground between fear of God's plan and boredom with your own. Or maybe you just want to know what's next in this journey with this great and gracious God. Now is your chance to take that scrap of paper in your hand and answer the question awaiting you: *What is one thing you are going to leave here?*

Throughout history, God has called his people to surrender to make His power known. Romans 9:16-21 says:

"It does not, therefore, depend on man's desire or effort, but on God's mercy. For the Scripture says to Pharaoh: 'I raised you up for this very purpose, that I might display my power in you and that my name might be proclaimed in all the earth.' Therefore God has mercy on whom he wants to have mercy, and he hardens whom he wants to harden. One of you will say to me: 'Then why does God still blame us? For who resists his will?' But who are you, O man, to talk back to God? 'Shall what is formed say to him who formed it, 'Why did you make me like this?'' Does the potter have the right to make out of the same lump of clay some pottery for noble purposes and some for common use?"

Our response to this *great* and *gracious* God should come from a heart of *humility* and *gratitude*. God does not need you. He graciously chooses to use you, if you're willing. Ephesians 2:10 says, *"For we are God's workmanship, created in Christ Jesus to do good works, which God prepared in advance for us to do."* God was gracious enough to prepare needs in this world, so we would have a purpose and an opportunity to serve him as He works in us.

The most common things we are called to surrender are the things we love most dearly or the things that we fear most deeply; at times they're linked. Abraham loved Isaac. We read in Genesis 22:2 *"Take your son, your only son, Isaac, whom you love, and go to the region of Moriah. Sacrifice him there as a burnt offering on one of the mountains I will tell you about."* Abraham surrendered; God blessed. Moses feared speaking to Pharaoh, Exodus 3:10 says, *"So now, go. I am sending you to Pharaoh to bring my people the Israelites out of Egypt."* Moses surrendered; God blessed. Solomon loved his riches and his wives without surrender. Looking back, he reminisces, *"Yet when I had surveyed all that my hands had done and what I had toiled to achieve, everything was meaningless, a chasing after the wind; nothing was gained under the sun"* (Ecclesiastes 2:11). Ultimately, Solomon did not surrender; ultimately, God did not bless. Jonah feared going to Nineveh, and he ran. God sent a storm and a fish, and Jonah surrendered. Remember, Jonah 2:8-9 says, *"Those who cling to worthless idols forfeit the grace that could be theirs. But I, with a song of thanksgiving, will sacrifice to you. What I have vowed I will make good. Salvation comes from the Lord."* Jonah surrendered; God blessed not only Jonah, but Nineveh as well.

Righteous people throughout history have realized that this life is worthless unless lived for Christ. Paul remarks in Philippians 1:21, *"For to me, to live is Christ and to die is gain."* He later says, *"What is more, I consider everything a loss compared to the surpassing greatness of knowing Christ Jesus my Lord, for whose sake I have lost all things. I consider them rubbish, that I may gain Christ"* (Philippians 3:8). Are you ready to join the ranks of the men and women who will someday take their crowns in Heaven and place them at the feet of Jesus? Are you ready to surrender? The first step in surrendering is getting on your knees, then praying and listening.

Maybe you have experienced supernatural work in your life over the past few weeks, and you are ready to leave something here. Now is your chance. If you know God is calling you to surrender something specific, go ahead and pray this first prayer.

Great and Gracious God, thank you for calling me to a life of "noble purposes." I confess that I have let the things I love most dearly and the things I fear most deeply get in the way of your plan for my life. I no longer want to follow the ways of this world, but like Jonah, and so many other people that you have called, I know you are calling me, and I surrender to your will.

Today I surrender my _____. *No matter what that means, take it and do something incredible with this life. Open doors for me to serve you for your glory. Fill me with your spirit and your power and use me, all of me. It's about you, God. I love you. Amen.*

If you are unsure what God is calling you to surrender, ask God to reveal to you if there is anything keeping you from Him. Pray this second prayer:

Great and Gracious God, I want your will for my life. Please reveal to me the things that keep me from you. Today, I surrender my life for your use, for your glory. Please fill me with your Spirit and power as

I serve you. Give me your heart for this world, and set me apart for "noble purposes." Thank you for everything you have in store for me. Like Jonah, do what it takes for me to live for you, bless me and bless others through me. It's all about you, God. I love you. Amen.

Do you want to respond to God in all the right ways? Take up a lifestyle of surrender, humility, listening and action. James 4:17 says, *"Anyone, then, who knows the good he ought to do and doesn't do it, sins."* Surrender humbly, listen and take action. Then see if God doesn't carry you through the storms, send you on unexpected ventures, transform entire cities through you, and reveal himself to you. God awaits your surrender. How will you respond?

DISCUSSION QUESTIONS

RUNNING THE OTHER DIRECTION

1. When you were a child, how did your mother call you to dinner?

_____

_____

_____

Read Jonah 1

2. The people of Nineveh worshiped multiple "gods," warred aggressively against their neighbors (including Israel), and treated their captives ruthlessly. Why would God send a prophet to people like this?

_____

_____

_____

3. When God calls, Jonah runs in the opposite direction. How did other prophets react to the call of God? (Is. 6:1-8; Ex. 4:10-16; Hos. 1:2-3)

_____

_____

_____

4. How did Jonah's response to God effect other people?

_____

_____

_____

5. The sailors were most likely animistic pagans (worshiping the spirits of the ocean, mountains, rivers, trees, etc). What did they learn about Yahweh on this day? How did they ultimately respond to Him (v. 16)?

_____

_____

_____

6. When Jonah ran, why didn't God assign a different prophet to complete His mission?

_____

_____

_____

7. Has God ever given you an assignment you refused to fulfill?

_____

_____

_____

8. What mission do you think God calling you to today?

_____

_____

_____

9. The theme of Jonah is the greatness and grace of God. We see His greatness in His dominance of the wind and waves, and His grace in the warning to the Ninevites, the sparing of the sailors, and the swallowing of Jonah. How do you want to respond to God's greatness and grace today?

_____

_____

_____

_____

INDIGESTION

1. When was the last time you were seasick?

_____

_____

_____

Read Jonah 1:17- 2:10

2. How long do you think Jonah was in the water before he was swallowed by the fish?

_____

_____

_____

3. How do you think Jonah felt at the moment he was swallowed?

     A. unconscious
     B. dazed
     C. fully alert

What makes you think this?

_____

_____

_____

4. If he was unconscious, Jonah may not have known where he was when he woke up inside the fish's belly. If that's the case, describe what he may have been thinking. Where might he have thought he was?

_____

_____

_____

5. Jonah 2:9 could better be translated, "May I sacrifice..." and "May I make good on what I vowed..." If that's the case, the verse is a hope or prayer rather than a proclamation. What do you think Jonah had vowed to do?

_____

_____

_____

6. In Jonah 1:1, what did Jonah do when God spoke? In Jonah 2:3, what did the fish do when God spoke?

_____

_____

_____

7. What do you think a human would look like after spending 36 to 48 hours enveloped in stomach acid?

_____

_____

_____

8. When have you felt like you were disobedient and paying for it?

_____

_____

_____

10. What's your next step with the Lord? How do you want to respond to Him so that you positively influence those around you?

_____

_____

_____

_____

A SECOND CHANCE

1. What are your favorite and least favorite big cities and why?

_____

_____

_____

Read Jonah 3

2. How has Jonah changed since chapter one?

_____

_____

_____

3. Why has Jonah changed?

_____

_____

_____

4. Why are the Ninevites so receptive to Jonah's message?

_____

_____

_____

5. List those who have changes of heart in this chapter:

_____

_____

_____

    a. What do these changes tell us about humans?

_____

    b. About humans who worship other gods?

_____

    c. About humans who claim to follow God?

_____

    d. About God Himself?

_____

6. When have you seen God give you a second chance?

_____

_____

_____

7. Have you ever resisted a second chance?

_____

_____

_____

8. Have you ever "put on sackcloth" in your heart over something you've done?

_____

_____

_____

9. Where are you right now?

    A. Like Jonah, I'm doing something I should have done in the first place.

    B. Like the Ninevites, I'm hearing God's call for the first time.

    C. Like God, I'm reconsidering a course of action I was going to take.

    D. Other:_____

10. What response do you want to make to God this week?

_____

_____

_____

_____

FRUSTRATED WITH GOD

1. Tell about a time when you were mad at your dad.

_____

_____

_____

Read Jonah 4

2. According to Jonah 4:2, why did Jonah originally run from God?

_____

_____

_____

3. Why is Jonah "displeased and angry"?

_____

_____

_____

4. What makes you mad at God?

_____

_____

_____

5. The verb "provided" is used three times in this chapter. What three items did God provide for Jonah? Why did He provide them? What purposes did these serve?

_____

_____

_____

6. Why does God show mercy to the Ninevites?

_____

_____

_____

7. What do you suppose happened to Jonah after Jonah 4:11?

_____

_____

_____

8. Despite all of his failings, Jonah influenced an entire city for good and for God. As a result of this study, what kind of influence would you like to have on your city? Spend a few minutes strategizing and then praying together about what you might do to influence the area in which you life.

_____

_____

_____

_____

Key Verses

Genesis 1:1	Exodus 3:8
Leviticus 20:7-8	Numbers 14:22-23
Deuteronomy 10:12-13	Joshua 11:23
Judges 17:6	Ruth 1:16
1 Samuel 15:22	2 Samuel 7:22-23
1 Kings 9:4-5	2 Kings 17:18-19; 17:22-23
1 Chronicles 29:12	2 Chronicles 7:14; 16:9
Ezra 7:10	Nehemiah 2:17
Esther 4:14	Job 23:10
Psalm 19:14	Proverbs 9:10
Ecclesiastes 1:14	Song of Songs 7:10
Isaiah 9:6-7	Jeremiah 8:11-12
Lamentations 3:22-23	Ezekiel 36:26
Daniel 4:17; 4:26	Hosea 3:1
Joel 2:13	Amos 8:11-12
Obadiah 15	Jonah 4:2
Micah 6:8; 7:18	Nahum 1:7-8
Habakkuk 3:2	Zephaniah 1:14-15
Haggai 1:8	Zechariah 8:3
Malachi 3:1	Matthew 28:18-20
Mark 10:45	Luke 19:10
John 20:30-31	Acts 1:8
Romans 1:16-17	1 Corinthians 6:19-20
2 Corinthians 5:20-21	Galatians 5:1
Ephesians 2:8-10; 4:1-3	Philippians 1:21
Colossians 3:1-2	1 Thessalonians 3:12-13
2 Thessalonians 2:15	1 Timothy 6:11-12
2 Timothy 3:16-17	Titus 1:5
Philemon 6	Hebrews 4:14-15
James 1:22	1 Peter 1:7
2 Peter 3:9-11	1 John 5:11-13
2 John 9	3 John 4
Jude 3	Revelation 1:19

JONAH
Campaign Resource Kit

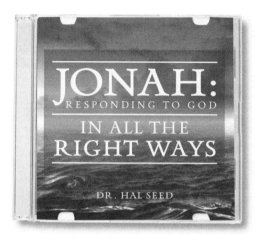

Resource kit includes everything your church will need to launch a four-week church-wide campaign on the Book of Jonah!

- **SERMON CD'S FOR**
    Jonah 1: Responding to God's Greatness
    Jonah 2: Responding to God's Correction
    Jonah 3: Responding to God's Grace
    Jonah 4: Responding to God's Correction (Again)

- **SERMON MANUSCRIPTS**

- **POWERPOINT PRESENTATIONS**

- **ARTWORK**

- **2 PROMOTIONAL VIDEOS TO EXCITE YOUR CHURCH ABOUT THE UPCOMING CAMPAIGN.**

FUTURE HISTORY
Campaign Resource Kit

Understanding the Book of Daniel and End Times Prophecy

The book of Daniel combines vivid history (Daniel in the Lion's Den, The Handwriting on the Wall, The Fiery Furnace) with precise predictions of the future of mankind. Future History is the perfect tool for personal or small group study. If you'd like to understand what's coming at the end of history, this is the book for you!

Resource kit includes everything your church will need to launch a six to twelve-week church-wide campaign on the Book of Daniel

- **9 SERMON CD'S FOR**
    - Daniel 1: The Making of Wise Men
    - Daniel 2: How to Hear From God
    - Daniel 3: When God Shows Up… Be Very Afraid
    - Daniel 4: When God Shows Up… Visions Get Bigger
    - Daniel 6: When God Shows Up… You've Passed the Test
    - Daniel 7: The Best (and Worst) Is Yet to Come
    - Daniel 8: The Ultimate Bad Guy at the End of Time
    - Daniel 9: The Prediction of Christ's First AND Second Comings
    - Daniel 10-12: The Final War of the World
- **10 SERMON MANUSCRIPTS**
- **POWERPOINT PRESENTATIONS**
- **ARTWORK**
- **2 PROMOTIONAL VIDEOS TO EXCITE YOUR CHURCH ABOUT THE UPCOMING CAMPAIGN.**

Additional Information & Resources
Available at **www.HalSeedBooks.com.**

THE GOD QUESTIONS

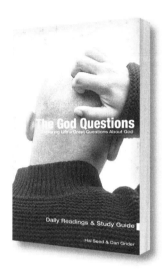
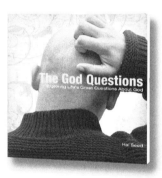

THE GOD QUESTIONS | THE GOD QUESTIONS GIFT EDITION

Everyone has questions about God. *The God Questions* answers 95% of the questions people ask about God. The book can be used for individual reading and study, as a small group curriculum and/or as a church-wide campaign. The Gift Edition is an excellent gift to give to seeking friends who have questions about God's existence, the Bible's reliability, the truth about other religions, and the problem of pain in the world.